Praise for "The Book on Small Business Ideas"

"Justin provides an outstanding framework for any successful outlier who wants to start their own small business.

Whether you are ready to go all in on your own small business or you want to start with a side hustle, you have to read this book."

Dr. John Shufeldt - *MD, JD, MBA, physician, multidisciplinary entrepreneur, author and speaker at www.johnshufeldt.com*

"There is no shortage of small business ideas or side hustles. But there is a shortage of people who have been able to find their own perfect idea and see it through to success.

The Book on Small Business Ideas is here to change that. You'll uncover your personal motivation and learn how to generate your own ideas. You'll evaluate success potential and then uncover the methods to stand out effectively in today's market. Make this your last year in the grind."

Nick Loper - *Chief Side Hustler at Side Hustle Nation*

sidehustlenation.com

"If you want to see a business idea or side hustle through to true success, be true to yourself and to your passion.

'The Book on Small Business Ideas' takes you on a deep journey that will set you up for legitimate, long-term success and freedom. Success in life is all about

building relationships and deepening connections...a topic near and dear to my heart. If you're looking to level up your life, this book is a must read."

Doug Sandler - *bestselling author and top-ranked podcast host at dougsandler.com*

"Breaking out of the traditional employment pattern is a dream for many people. Justin's first book provided inspiration and fuel for my personal journey.

Now, he's back with The Book on Small Business Ideas and has completely amped it up. I dare you to pick up this book and not take action on the side hustle or small business of your dreams."

Mary Cheyne - *bestselling author, MBA, award-winning communicator, and president of Magnetic Podium, LLC*

Praise for "Leave the Grind Behind"

"Leave the Grind Behind is an exceptional, actionable, and unique look at how to successfully quit your day job and follow your passions. It will prime you for repeated success while also maintaining a balanced life.

I've been able to personally see Justin Gesso's plan in action and the fantastic results it has yielded. If you're ready to quit your day job, make more money, follow your passions, and be in control of your time, I enthusiastically recommend this book for you."

Elena Pezzini, PhD - *#1 Bestselling Author and Certified Life & Financial Coach*

"Justin Gesso maps out how therapeutic practices, Dialectical Behavior Therapy, and Scripting all in the concept of mindset. If you want to leave any or all of your ineffective habits or lifestyle behind, follow the steps outlined in Leave the Grind Behind. You will be living a new fulfilling life, achieving your personal best."

Marcia J. Murphy, Ph.D - *Licensed Clinical Psychologist*

"Move over Tim Ferriss, there's a refreshed approach to unshackling yourself from the grueling busy-work of the grind.

Having taken many steps to minimize the impact of wasted time, I came ready to hear what your approach would be. I found the basis in mental energy to be right on target--the minute anyone puts themselves in a position to want change, the first challenge is always overcoming their own psychological barriers.

Affirmations tied to habits tied to goals...you've covered critical ground to make positive change.

Once I made it through, I found myself itching to do the actions. I couldn't wait to hit the street!"

Matthew Hart - *Author and CTO Arise Virtual Solutions*

"Leave the Grind Behind dives deep into the tactical steps and actions you need to start taking today to find yourself making money on your own quickly. Having left my corporate job to run a successful business of my own, I will tell you...take this model and execute on it."

Ashok Reddy - *Founder and CEO of BETSOL*

"This is it. Leave the Grind Behind shows you the way to repeatedly achieve success on your own terms. These are the exact practices I've used to achieve extraordinary results in multiple business."

Mark Ferguson - *Owner of Multi-Million Dollar Real Estate Businesses and Bestselling Author of InvestFourMore*

"Justin Gesso is the secret sauce behind a lot of successful people, myself included. This book is to the point and an easy read. Lots of highly actionable stuff here.

Do it! This will get you motivated and on the right path to doing something big in your life."

Ben Leybovich - *Real Estate Investor and Entrepreneur*

What Justin Gesso's Readers Have to Say

"If this doesn't leave you motivated and ready to tackle your life head on then I don't know what will. It is filled with great advice and guidance to get you out of your humdrum job and into your own successful business! Do yourself a favour and read this book, it will change your life."

"Fabulous read with brilliant points to make big adjustments to improve your life."

"Today, I decided to quit the grind...I want to thank you for the work you do."

"OH! I started teaching art again and my first class was a huge success. I am starting to pick up commissions (I have three) and I have been taking courses from people I admire on the business of art. I even have a mentor!"

"I've been meaning to email you and tell you that I QUIT MY JOB!!! I have six months salary saved up and am just two weeks out of the six-figure corporate hell hole... Thanks for all your motivational emails. They did much to push me off the fence."

"This book changed my life. I'm already going into business for myself, I feel less stressed, have been spending more time with my family. I feel free."

"I have read other books with similar ideas, but Justin's book has actually motivated me to action."

"I needed to read a positive, uplifting, and well written book, with ideas for my future and where I may be going. There are other reads with this concept, but Justin Gesso hit a home run...thank you for leaving me and others with ideas I can use."

"I've had a comfortable job earning pretty good money and could have stayed here until my end, but I'd always hankered to run a backpacker hostel in a crazy busy place. Sooo...next month I'm off to SE Asia to do just that."

"This book changed my view on the 9-5. I was already miserable at my office job and Justin's words just solidified it. Last week, I put in my 2 weeks and decided to go into freelance writing! My boss was so sad to see me go that they are hiring me to do off site projects!"

"Your words are working so thank you, truly."

The Book on Small Business Ideas

Level up your mindset, launch high-cash-flow money machines, and finally quit your job this year without the financial risk.

JUSTIN GESSO

First Edition

Authored by Justin Gesso

Foreword by Greg Helmerick

Edited by Greg Helmerick

Cover Design by Carol Scott

The author has made best efforts to determine the sources of all quotes contained herein.

This one is for you readers out there who take action. I wouldn't be back if it wasn't for unbelievable feedback and success stories I've received from you.

Table of Contents

Foreword

Greg Helmerick

I was born with a grammatical spoon in my mouth. For as long as I can remember, reading, writing, and grammar came easy to me. So it only made sense that I should pursue a degree in English Writing. I did so while working a full-time job, but once I had my degree, I didn't know what to do with it. I always enjoyed my natural talent for grammar, but I just didn't have the techniques and fundamentals in place that would help me build a career out of that talent.

Then, Justin called me. Justin and I have been friends for over 10 years, and after abruptly deciding to leave the corporate world forever, he wrote *Leave the Grind Behind*. He needed an editor, and it just so happened he knew someone with the right skills!

After a brief discussion about the terms and book's focus, I agreed and started grinding. Two things happened during the process. First, I realized (again) how much I love working with grammar. I love cleaning it up, improving clarity, enhancing readability, and striving to perfect it. Second, I learned valuable techniques and habits. Justin's methods were actionable, straightforward, and sensible, and I started seeing ways to apply game-changing practices in my own life. In a word, Justin gave me the belief that I could turn one of my most valuable skills into a lucrative, scalable side hustle.

The opportunity to edit *Leave the Grind Behind* was just the start. In no time, I had become the published editor of a successful, highly rated international bestseller. I was finally "out there," and that visibility started leading to additional opportunities. Justin—and his networking techniques—helped me grow my name and business. And since *Leave the Grind Behind* was published just over a year ago, I've done professional editing as a side hustle for eight books (including this one) and have an ongoing editing contract with a major blog, all of which has resulted in five-figure earnings this year alone.

You're now holding or viewing Justin's next big project, and I couldn't be more proud of it...or him. Building on the practices in *Leave the Grind Behind*, The Book on Small Business Ideas will inspire you and spark your journey.

Most books in this space are written by someone who had a winning-lotto-ticket idea, but how many of us can really hope to realize the same success? Justin doesn't teach you how to get rich quickly—he teaches you how to get rich correctly. His books provide sustainable and accessible methods for the rest of us. Indeed, success is a foundation with many pillars, and each pillar, from mindset to networking to health, must be solid. Justin helps you build solid pillars through actionable success principles.

My editing career is just getting started, and I owe it all to Justin. None of this would have been possible had I not followed his principles, implemented his networking techniques, and put his daily habits into place.

I hope this book gives you that extra push you may need to follow your entrepreneurial dreams.

My goal is to ensure books with my name on them are as free of grammatical errors as possible. If you find any errors in this book...or if you want to shower me with praise or need a copy editor of your own, feel free to email me: greg@helmerick.com.

Introduction: Your New Lifestyle Awaits

Starting your own business is a big deal! Just by purchasing this book, you're showing some serious bravery. You're showing passion, ambition, and desire. You want to make something happen in your life. You don't want life to happen to you.

Creating your own business is risky. Even if you're just creating a side hustle, you're risking the loss of your valuable time; you're risking putting work into something that takes a lot of energy; and you're risking your pride. Everyone has the same thoughts. "What if I fail? What if I lose money? What if no one likes what I sell, produce, or do?"

But I have a feeling you picked up this book because you've started to realize that playing it safe is far more risky. You are not content being a cog in someone else's design. You do not like chugging away—day after day—just to be average. You are pouring the majority of your time and energy into someone else's company...someone else's dream. You are doing what most other people do, and you've become a blur.

Your job defines you, but it's time to turn the tables. It's time to design your new life and create the money-making machines to support it. It's time for you to control your income—and stop letting it control you.

This book will get you there.

It will show you how to make much more money on your own, spend time how you want, build a simple business, and quit your day job. We'll do this without putting you at risk financially and without the complexity many people associate with running a business.

Alright—before we move on, let me address the three "buts" I hear most often...

BUT starting a small business takes a lot of time, money, and financial risk!

America used to be the land of opportunity; now, we have a *world* of opportunity! Technology has given us all an incredible gift. All of the systems we need to run a successful business are readily—and often freely—available. We can plug and play to reach massive global audiences like never before.

And yes, launching a small business takes time. But if you do this properly—with the right introspection and the right mental approach—you'll pick something you're excited to do! Something you love. When you are brimming with excitement, you'll have no problem waking up a little earlier. You won't want to watch that TV show. You'll want to chase down your dreams and create a better life for yourself.

I personally had all of the time, money, and risk excuses too. But once I found my passion, it was simply a matter of executing efficiently.

In this book, I'll show you the tools and processes to make room for greatness. And best of all, I'll show you how to do this so your effort is up front, while your fruits last for years to come.

BUT running a business is complicated!

Many businesses are complicated. Complex processes, custom systems, layers of human resources, and teams of accountants abound! But who said businesses need to be complex? The best small businesses are simple! This is why I love the term "money machine." It embodies simplicity.

- What about the writer who makes $15,000 per month from his blog?
- What about another author who consistently makes over $40,000 per month from a book he wrote five years ago?
- What about the guy who bought rental properties—without any of his own money—and was able to quit his W-2 job just three years later?
- What about the guy who makes $8 million per year by providing a service that connects software engineers with contract jobs?

They all have extremely simple business models. Complexity is not a prerequisite for success. This book will help you avoid the complexities and find the simplest path possible.

And finally...BUT it takes someone special to stand out, and I'm not special!

If you picked up this book, I think there's a good chance you are special. You are striving for more. You're ready to take control. You're ready to level up your life.

The only thing holding you back is a lack of action. If you finish this book, put it on the shelf, and never take action as a result, we'll never know your potential.

Many people dream of levelling up and having the life they want. Will you be one of the few who take action?

Most people won't. Most people won't turn their dreams into reality. And, most people won't stick with their ideas long enough. But I can help. This book will help you uncover your true drive. You will want to pour your passion into this. You will want to outhustle the competition. You will have the tools to stand out.

No more BUTS

I've filled this book with exercises to help you find your passion, generate momentum, and stand out from the crowd. The concepts in this book won't put you at risk, and they won't be complicated. So, the only thing you stand to lose is opportunity.

People are taking action every day...now it's your turn.

Why You Must Create Businesses

Perhaps you want to live in the best cities in the world. Perhaps you want to spend months at the beach. Perhaps you want to change your city's culture. Or, maybe you want to drive global change. Whatever it is, you've decided it's time to work on what you want to, when you want to, and where you want to.

It's also time to create. Creative expression is one of the most deeply satisfying activities humans can undertake. It allows us to live authentically. When was the last time you were so engrossed in an idea that time disappeared? You woke up excited to start. You forgot to eat lunch. And before you realized it, the sun had set. It was all you could think about—you were deeply obsessed.

You were creating. You were in love with your work, and it was immensely satisfying.

Have you lost that excitement that comes from creation? Most of us have. Over time, work, obligations, and life creep in. They get in the way. Your creative feelings, opportunities, and passion fade. But they didn't need to.

Whatever you really want from life, there is almost no chance you'll get it following the standard path. Rather, that path will almost certainly shackle you to an unremarkable life. Future generations—including your grandchildren—won't talk about you. You may not even find your day worth talking about. On the standard path, you'll turn in each night having left not even the smallest mark on the world.

But it's easier than ever to change your course. We all have the ability to create and to reach millions of people like never before. It's time.

A Rude Awakening

Most exceptional people I know have experienced a traumatic event. Tough moments seem to force life-altering perspectives.

It's as though we all begin our adult lives by walking down a path, heads held high, our vision clear, our steps confident and controlled. We know where we're going. Our teachers, family members, and others have all pointed us down *that* path. The standard path.

Without realizing it, our gaze drops, and we stare at our feet—so much so that we begin missing what's around us. Heads drooped, we progress in assembly line fashion. The world and our role in it narrows. Our experiences contract and become less memorable.

But sometimes, something violent and unexpected happens. Without warning, one of us is struck. Something crashes across the path and takes a poor soul with it. Those around recoil in horror and droop closer to the security of the path. But what about the one who was struck? After the moment of shock, they look up. They see the world around, the world they had stopped seeing. They see the sky. Their head is ringing and their body is battered, yet their excitement and happiness is palpable. The path no longer matters; this is the first day of the rest of their life.

My moment occurred on an otherwise peaceful, typical, narrow-world day. I was sitting in my home office, working through email, and droning through a conference call. I'd grown accustomed to the daily grind of my six-figure job. A great cup of home-brewed coffee was never far away, and I didn't have to worry about wearing a tie...or even shoes. My dog generally lay at my feet, happy to keep me company all day. To anyone watching, my day might have seemed pretty envious.

But that day decided to take a left turn and jolt me out of the grind. I was about to get knocked down.

Flu-like symptoms crept on quickly. I began losing concentration and feeling nauseous. I excused myself from the conference call to lie down on the floor. While I was fine mere moments earlier, I suddenly didn't have the power to get up and leave the room.

The whole experience struck me as entirely unreal. I had never felt so horribly sick so quickly. I had no reason to suspect any health issues. I was young and fit. I worked out regularly and ate well. But as my symptoms progressed, my ability to reflect on the situation faded. Everything intensified rapidly and showed no signs of slowing down.

The room was now spinning violently. I was pinned to the floor. I don't exactly remember what happened next, but I must have managed to call my wife. The next thing I remember is being upstairs in the bedroom. But my problems continued to escalate. The best way I can describe the feeling is to say it's probably how you'd feel if you downed 20 shots of tequila in under ten minutes.

At this point, I only have a handful of memories in still-frame fashion. They start with my wife somehow dragging me into the car and rushing me to a nearby urgent-care center. I remember dropping out of the car as she opened the door. She feared I was having a heart attack. While I was rolled in on a stretcher, the doctors assessed me but could not determine the issue and could not stop the symptoms. I needed to be transported.

Once I arrived at a full hospital, I received medication that actually seemed to help. And then with a great sigh of relief, I simply shut down. When I woke—innumerable hours later—the ordeal was over. But it's impact wasn't.

Whatever happened, it was enough to jar my consciousness loose. I had been knocked off the path, and I felt as though I was seeing the world for the first time. I evaluated everything about my life. I thought about my family, my ambitions, and what was important to me. I saw my future. I knew what would happen if I stayed on the path. See, I had already achieved what the world considers standard goals at a young age. I was working for a big company, earning good money, and by all external appearances, had made it. But this event made me question everything.

> "What individuals with huge egos don't realize is that failure is a gift."
> ~John Shufeldt, Ingredients of Outliers~

Did I really want to end up like the lifers at my company—at any company? What was I missing out on? What *would* I be missing out on? Life felt big and full. But work dominated it...work I was doing for someone else...work that was forgettable and inconsequential. At the end, it wasn't what mattered to me, so why was I spending most of my waking hours, most of my thoughts, and most of my energy on it?

I was on the path everyone told me to walk. And I wasn't just walking on it...I was running! Wherever that path was going, I was determined to get there quickly. But everyone was wrong about the path. And I was wrong too. *I was on the wrong path.*

My event was minor. I get that. I know others who have experienced events that were far more traumatic. They have been diagnosed with life-long conditions or have lost loved ones. But my event was enough for me, and for that, I'm thankful.

Despite countless appointments, MRIs, tests, and scans, doctors never did figure out what happened or if it would recur. Whether right or wrong, I'm convinced this event was the physical manifestation of being *out of alignment with my true self.* If you put enough stress on any system, it breaks. Removing that stress, I decided, was a matter of living authentically. I made my own recovery plan. I needed to pursue my interests and passions. Instead of working for money, I needed money to work for me.

What followed was simple. I redirected my energy toward engineering life the way I wanted. Within a couple of months, I executed on it, handed in my resignation, and never looked back. In fact, the grass is so much greener I've *vowed* to never go back. I'll do whatever it takes to avoid a standard job.

Here's a quick overview of what I've accomplished since leaving the grind:

- 2x'd my six-figure corporate income within just one and a half years.
- 2x'd my net worth within two years.
- Worked ground level with numerous multi-million dollar startups, integral to their launch and growth.

…all while working fewer hours, being in charge of my time, and most importantly, enjoying what I do. None of this would have happened this fast—or at all—on the standard path.

And since publishing the 1st edition of *Leave the Grind Behind* almost exactly one year ago, the ride has only improved. That book went on to be a bestseller. I've made many wonderful connections as a result. It has allowed me to achieve a personal goal of positively impacting tens of thousands of people. My real estate portfolio is up over $800,000 (all of which happened in about three years). A couple of the businesses that were starting at the time I wrote *Leave the Grind Behind* have successfully grown, beating goals I set for them. And most recently, I added a gorgeous Tesla Model S to my garage. Can't complain about that!

Is my journey over? No…far from it. I continue to feel more successful, savvy, and happy. I'm currently under contract with a partner to acquire and reposition a 60-unit apartment building. I'm about to sell a product at scales many people only dream of. I'm fortunate to spend time on fulfilling projects I enjoy, such as writing this book. My network and small-business opportunities continue to expand. I'm able to use my time flexibly, leaving me more time to enjoy my family.

But I still feel like I'm just scratching the surface. I love the path I'm on yet know there's so much more. If anything has become clear on this journey it's that the people and relationships are what matter. So I'm expanding my goal of reaching people. I want to reach millions of people with messages they can relate to and be inspired by. I hope this book is a big step in that direction. And specifically, I hope it gives *you* the tools and inspiration to set yourself free and realize the exact life you desire.

> "Thriving in your professional life is about more than just coping through these traumatic events—it is about turning tragedy around and making it work for you."
> ~Is Workplace Trauma the Key to Success? Cramer Institute~

As I write this, I wonder if my awakening was actually that rude. It seems like it may have been the best thing that could've happened to me. Maybe doing something big requires some degree of trauma. Maybe it takes a massive impact to knock you off the rails. Maybe not.

What about you? If you picked up this book, I suspect you're ready to take control. Whatever your situation, whatever your cause, let's make sure you're not just along for the ride. Let's put you in the driver's seat. If you want to share your story with me, I'd love to hear it. Email me at justin@justingesso.com.

The 52x Concept

Following my "rude" awakening, I knew I needed a framework in place to avoid losing the feelings, perspective, and energy I gained. The standard path is magnetic and tries to draw you back in. I created the 52x concept to challenge its power.

Creating a better life for yourself starts with deliberate action. Creating a small business or side hustle is no exception. While there are shortcuts and best practices, make no mistake about it: you are going to sacrifice something now in order to create the life you want. Maybe your sacrifice is as small as giving up TV time. Maybe it means getting up at 4 a.m. for the next six months. Whatever it is, you will modify something you're currently doing to change your results and outcomes. You need to constantly remind yourself to look up from the path.

Deciding to put in the work and make sacrifices is a moment-by-moment choice. Do you hit snooze, or do you get up and exercise? Do you stay late at a job you dislike, or do you go home to have dinner with your family? Do you make that important sales call you've been dreading, or do you keep flipping through social media?

To help myself through these choices, I began placing them in the context of one year—52 weeks. I think, "If I choose this activity:"

- Will I be better off in 52 weeks?
- Will I remember this activity in 52 weeks?

Where will your current activities take you? If you finish this book, do the exercises, and implement at least some of it, do you expect to be better off in 52 weeks? What if you set it down and binge-watch more of that familiar sitcom, the one so many people say wasn't worth finishing?

The 52x concept doesn't judge your choices. It is simply a checkpoint. Rather than plodding through life on forgetful cruise control, stop and question your choices. Perhaps the best choice is to relax, unwind, and watch that sitcom again. But make that time investment a deliberate choice rather than a default one. Don't let your choices own you. Own them...and do your future self proud.

So what is 52x? It's a reminder. It's motivation. It's a lifestyle and a guide. It ensures you get the most out of today and the future. It ensures life is not a blur of average.

Cogs vs Grinders

If you read my book *Leave the Grind Behind*, you will be familiar with a couple of terms I use: Cogs and Grinders. If not, here's a primer. (To get a personal sense of these terms, head over to the Cog vs Grinder Quiz at justingesso.com/quiz.)

Cogs

If you're a Cog, you're mired "in the grind." You're spending eight or more hours per day, Monday through Friday, working for *someone else's* dreams, passions, and riches. Your efforts make millions...for someone else.

For Cogs, the term "grind" means monotony. It means life is a blur. The weekend is over; now, it's back to the grind. Even if you earn a solid six-figure salary, own a nice house, and are contributing to your 401K, spending your time working primarily for someone else leaves you feeling empty. You're on the path.

Grinders

If you're a Grinder, you work hard for your *personal* purpose and goals—not for someone else's. Make no mistake, to leave the grind behind, you need to work hard. Even so, you love it because you're working for *you*.

As a Grinder, you spend your valuable time building your own legacy and unique imprint on this world. We live in what Success Magazine calls the "You Economy." That is such an empowering term. Like never before, technology and people are primed to enable individuals to monetize abilities and reach a global audience. As a Grinder, you have the power to capitalize on this and create the life you want.

Transitioning from Cog to Grinder

As someone begins taking ownership for their life, they often experience an awakening. For most of your professional life, someone has told you what to do and how to get there. This causes your life to lose meaning. The first time something doesn't go right, you can simply give up and say *that other person's plan didn't work.*

But what happens when you're in charge? If it's your goal and your plan, there's only one place to point the finger. You're responsible. You make it work. You enjoy the results. You adapt on the fly. Life completely changes. You're no longer along for the ride; you move to the driver's seat.

What Exactly Is a Small Business?

Most people have preconceptions about what it means to run a business. Whether you have a store owner, mad scientist, or tycoon in mind, let's formulate a solid definition to ensure you have the right concept.

In the United States, the Small Business Administration officially manages the term "small business." But if you read their literature, you'll find a lengthy definition appended by a *very* lengthy standards document. Reading through it will likely leave you with more questions than answers.

So let me jump right to the meat of it and define "small business" as I want you to know it for this book. A small business is simply *an entity organized to generate a profit*. Taking that one step further, I want your small business to generate money for you so you can realize your life goals.

What you don't see in my definition is any assumption of size or complexity. I don't care if your small business is a side hustle, self employment, or an organization of 50. Unbelievable results can be achieved from any construct. Value is independent of size and complexity. Can you make it big with a big idea? Can you make it big with several small ideas? Yes and yes.

When it comes to owning a small business, what do you think of? Do you imagine owning a small specialty store in your town? Do you imagine selling a product online? Maybe you think of running a professional firm with 15 engineers that will soon grow to 500.

The small business you create is there to generate income, help you fulfill your goals, and increase your freedom. Nothing more. Creating a small business doesn't need to be daunting or overwhelming. In its most basic form, it's exciting, achievable, and liberating. It's a machine designed to advance your personal agenda.

To reinforce the idea that in order to achieve your goals, you don't necessarily need to create something big and complex, consider:

- The average American has one income stream...and seven lines of debt.
- The average American millionaire has seven income streams.

It's tough to source the exact facts, but you'll see these figures regularly discussed. Whether perfectly precise or not, they elegantly highlight the principles of this section. Grinders layer numerous recurring income streams and businesses over time, building their wealth and independence.

Whatever you imagine, don't let someone's definition of "creating a business" hold you back. Likewise, don't let someone else's definition water down your massive goals either. All I ask is that you keep an open mind and move forward, taking the necessary action to add your next income stream.

Is Creating a Business for You?

I hope this book causes you to become as addicted to creating and running new business ideas as I am. I hope you learn to see it as a game. And once you understand the playing field, I hope you find it exciting and rewarding. I hope you want to get new businesses and ideas out there as much as possible.

For the right people, I believe the enjoyment of creating businesses is so great that you never see those people stop. Rather, they are constantly out there trying something new. The benefits are much greater than money alone. This is why you don't see people who have made it big resting on their winnings.

So are you one of these people? Do you have what it takes? Should you get off the path? Let's find out:

- Do you have a desire to create and make an impact?
- Are you repulsed by being average?
- Are you willing to identify personal weaknesses and constantly learn?
- Do you have the ability to exude passion, enthusiasm, and obsession?
- Do you see the many things that go right in a day (as opposed to the many things that go wrong)?

Together, we can fill in a lot of blanks and round out a lot of rough edges, but look hard at that list. If you're missing that foundation, this book may not be for you. But, if those words describe you, welcome aboard. You're going to make this happen.

How to Use this Book

I cover a lot of concepts, exercises, and minutiae in this book. As you're going through it, keep a pen and notebook handy.

Additionally, I've prepared guides, worksheets, and other important downloads that you can grab at…

justingesso.com/52x

CHAPTER 1

The Plan

Before getting into the meat of this book, I think it's important to lay out the big picture. I want to clarify right up front that this book is not going to walk you through filling out tax forms, registering trade names, or completing many of the other simple "paperwork" items that people worry about when starting a business. If you're thinking at that level, you're going to become a small-business statistic. As you work through this book, you'll understand why considering the minutiae as secondary is key to succeeding.

Rather, this book aims big. You're going to generate so much passion and momentum that those little details won't matter. So how do you fuel the sort of velocity and power that steamrolls through hurdles, failure, naysayers, doubt, and paperwork?

The answer is to get introspective. You might expect a "small-business idea" book to give you a giant list of prepped-and-ready business ideas, but that would be a recipe for failure. So rather than putting you in a position to fail, I'm going to help you become an idea factory. To be successful, you need to become the catalyst.

With this in mind, this book doesn't just give you a plan...it takes you on a journey.

The 4-Part Journey

Part I: Lifestyle Design

It's all about you. We need to dive deep into what makes you tick. We'll get into your goals and motivations and create your master plan for your life...not just for your business.

I owe my current situation to the massive library of success books and coaching programs that I devoured after my rude awakening. None of those provided concrete steps for doing what I did—they provided much more. They completely opened my mind and changed my perspective on what it means to be successful. I'll bring the best of those books and programs to you in this section.

Part II: Foundation

After going through self-discovery exercises and being honest with yourself, it's time to address common reasons I see people fail...regardless of how great their business ideas are. In this section, we'll dive into your people network, free up time, free up money, and get you obsessed with achieving what you want in life.

You don't want weaknesses to come back and haunt you, so we'll establish plans and habits to address them. This section will almost certainly push you out of your comfort zone.

Part III: Selection

By this point, you should be brimming with ideas and enthusiasm. It's time to expand, evaluate, and dissect. We'll go through idea generation, evaluation using a detailed tool, and a final-preparation checklist. You'll come to the table with many great ideas, then weed them down to the select few destined to actually make you money quickly. After all, we want you to *start a business and profit this year.*

Part IV: Launch

Ideas—even great ideas—are worthless without execution. So I'm not going to leave you hanging with *just* great business ideas. You've done too much work, and you need to see it through. This phase will get you on the scene with a bang and ensure you follow through with the execution needed to start generating real cash and real profits. We'll establish an action plan, dive into marketing, sell before ready, launch, beat the competition, and close by establishing a habit of continuous improvement.

You will have the blueprint for launching a successful business and profiting thereby. Once you get your business in a steady state, it's my hope you'll be dying to go back to page one and start all over again with business number two.

Bonus: Going Big

I'll admit—it was hard for me to stop writing this book. I enjoyed it immensely. So, I made a last-minute decision. I decided to include a chapter on going big with your ideas. If you know your idea will cause you to reach your goals, I'll cover the best ways to go all in.

How Much Time, Money, and Effort Do I Need?

At this point, you might be saying, "This all sounds great, but my life is already overflowing...I don't have time to think, let alone start a business." Maybe your time is already maxed out by your job and family. And maybe you're shackled by more than just time. Maybe you picked this book up because you're looking for a way out of financial trouble. Maybe, at the end of the day, you're mentally and physically exhausted. How are you supposed to stay motivated to put in the effort?

Look, I faced the same challenges. I had a demanding day job. I had a young family, and I wasn't going to sacrifice my time with them. We were a single-income household, so the money pressure was there too. I couldn't fail.

It's important to acknowledge your doubts in these areas, but don't worry. This book assumes you must overcome some or all of these challenges. These are major yet common hurdles. And that's exactly why this book addresses them head on. This is why we spend time on you first and the business second. By taking this approach, you'll become obsessed. You'll stop watching TV. You'll get up a little earlier. And we'll go through exercises to truly help you maximize time and money in your life. My guess is you'll be shocked by what you're able to accomplish.

Balance and Success

I commonly see people succeeding in one area of life at the expense of other areas. Many people chase money at the expense of their relationships, often only realizing there is a problem when it's too late. We should strive to get the most out of life in all areas that are important to us. Having a business will afford us this ability in ways a regular job cannot.

While the money is great, the real benefit it offers is financial freedom. Financial freedom affords you the ability to spend time the way you want, not the way the standard path requires. How do you *want* to spend your time?

You're here to grow a business and build your future, so you may be surprised by—and tempted to skip over—the broader introspection sections within this book. But if aspects of your life are out of whack or cluttered, your ability to succeed will suffer. It's that simple. Just as you can become trapped in a corporate job, you can also become caught in a trap of your own creation.

So while you might initially be surprised to see references to non-business items in this book, I want you to realize life and business are one in the same. Living authentically will get you what you want from life. Designing your business without respect to your bigger life picture will not.

A Note on Happiness

We live in a time when we are surrounded by imagery, media, and pressure to attain and flaunt material wealth. That is, we are bombarded by a prevailing image of success that is associated with bling. While this self-centered approach, one that's focused on accumulating fancy stuff, is magnified by social media...it's not new. Pressure to keep up with the Joneses has been a misguided trap for far longer than social media has been around.

The reality of that material lifestyle, however, is becoming more and more clear.

I raise this issue because you are about to spend a lot of time defining how you want your future to look. So here's a warning—don't use someone else's showy lifestyle as a guide for what will make you happy. Don't let the news, social media, or me to tell you what you should want. Instead, dig into yourself and think about times in your life when you were truly happy. Use your own happiness as a guide to develop an intrinsic orientation rather than an extrinsic one.

You are going to devote time and energy to building a successful business: do it to make yourself happy.

What's the Deal with Lists?

In the exercises throughout this book, I will ask you to list numerous items, even though I only want you to select a couple of ideas. Why is this?

One of the best coaches I had was a list fanatic. He never explained why, but I began to understand the power of lists after I finally stopped resisting and started creating big lists anytime I faced a problem. Let me explain.

If you want to hit three goals, I will ask you to list 30 goals. If I want you to run with one business idea, I may ask you to come up with 100 ideas. Here are the two key reasons:

- Thinking of three or ten items may be easy, but getting into the double and triple digits will force you to really think and be creative. You're more likely to spend adequate time on the task and think outside the box.

- When you share your ideas, people will inevitably start poking holes in them and shoot them down. You'll ignore some of this criticism, but certain criticism may be valid. What happens if you just have 3 ideas, and for valid reasons, all 3 are shot down? Many people give up. We don't want that. If, on the other hand, you have a huge list of ideas, you won't be as emotionally tied to them. You'll be much more likely to take criticism constructively and press forward because your emotional investment is low enough that you won't feel defeated. You just move to the next.

Big lists have worked magic for me, and I want you to push yourself to meet my targets for each list. I promise you'll learn to love big lists.

One important tip: engage other people in your list-making efforts. If you need to make a list of your top 30 strengths, ask others for help. They may see opportunities you don't.

Objectives

Alright, it's time for your first exercise. Be clear about why you're here. Why did you pick up this book?

> "The individual who wants to reach the top in business must appreciate the might and force of habit. He must be quick to break those habits that can break him—and hasten to adopt those practices that will become the habits that help him achieve the success he desires."
>
> ~J. Paul Getty~

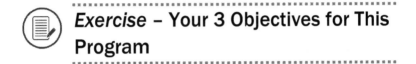

Exercise – Your 3 Objectives for This Program

Don't worry, these objectives will change and morph as we progress. You'll go through much more in-depth discovery of your purpose, mission, and goals. But let's start with you giving me a rough idea of why you're here.

What are your three objectives for the next 52 weeks? In your own words, why did you start this book? Pull out a notebook and write those objectives down. Capture the energy and excitement you have. Lock in what brought you here in the first place.

Part I

Lifestyle Design

Part I Introduction

Why do you want to start a small business? Why do you want to be independent and in control? Unlike anything else, being able to generate your own income in a satisfying manner gives you incredible freedom and allows you to live a lifestyle of your design. So let's ensure you know what you really want out of this journey.

The chapters in Part I will ensure you've thought out your motivations completely. You've spent enough time designing your life to suit your work. It's time to flip things around and design work to suit your life. Let's figure out where the grass is greener for you.

CHAPTER 2

You First, Business Second

Goals

- Commit to yourself and this program
- Create a baseline measurement of your current success and life satisfaction
- Determine your mission in life
- Uncover your key values and how they affect your success and actions
- **Action:** Start using the daily and monthly worksheets at *justingesso.com/52x*

Commitment

Alright, it's time to start the best year of your life! Not only will you start a profitable business (or businesses) this year, but you will also align your activities with what makes you personally tick. You'll round out your life and ensure your business is built upon a solid personal foundation.

Having your own businesses—your own money-making machines—affords you the ability to live a life of your design. Let's kick things off by helping you determine your big-picture purpose and mission. Once you understand your personal mission, we'll fit in your business mission...not the other way around.

> "Passion is one of the greatest forces that unleashes creativity, because if you're passionate about something, then you're more willing to take risks."
> ~Yo-yo Ma~

 ## *Exercise – Commit*

You are responsible for getting what you want out of life. You are responsible for determining your purpose and legacy. You are about to take an awesome journey. In one year, you will be in a completely different place. Your first step is to cement your commitment to the life you want. Read, sign, and date each of the following commitments.

Commitment One

I commit to using this book and earnestly completing the exercises. I will be honest and introspective with myself. I will achieve things I never have before.

_____   _____

Signature   *Date*

Commitment Two

I commit to earning more money, having more free time, having better relationships, and getting what I want from life.

_____ _____
Signature   *Date*

Commitment Three

I commit to making changes to my mindset, to how I interact with people, to how I execute, and to my daily routine and habits.

_____ _____
Signature   *Date*

Commitment Four

I commit to doing hard work now knowing my better life is right around the corner.

_____ _____
Signature   *Date*

Mission

Successful businesses define their purpose—you should too. To achieve incredible results, CEOs must define the purpose of their business, and they do that through a mission statement. A mission statement is similarly important to your own success. You are the CEO of your life. Define your *personal* mission.

Your mission statement will serve as the basis for how you lead your entire life. In this way, having a mission is incredibly liberating. Your mission statement serves as a guidepost. Your decisions, habits, and actions become easy. Either you're supporting your mission...or you're not. Your goals and effort to achieve them will be aligned with your mission statement.

So let's put your personal mission statement together. Start with these steps:

1. List your top skills and traits.

What do you consistently excel at? What did you do well in school? What do you do well in the workplace? What are your strengths? Examples might include broader areas like writing, art, mathematics, sales, mentoring, motivating, relationships, or even physical traits like strength and speed. Make a list of at least 30 items.

2. Determine the value you would love to provide.

How do you want to fit into the world? What do you want to improve? How would you like to reach people so they become aware of the traits you already listed? How is the world better with you in it? List at least 5 ideas.

3. Determine which people you want to impact.

Maybe you want to be a big part of your local community (thousands) or a city or region (millions), or perhaps you want to make a massive impact on the globe (billions). Do some research on your target locations and demographics. Study the sort of people you want to impact and come up with a specific group or number.

4. List your favorite activities.

This list will often overlap with your top skills and traits, which is great. If you excel at something, wouldn't it be great if you could spend more time on activities that utilize your excellence? Examples of activities you enjoy might include programming, working with your hands, making music, writing, fixing cars, cycling, speaking, or leading. List at least 30 items.

5. Bring it all together.

Don't worry we'll continue to refine your mission statement, but let's get started by putting pen to paper. Extract the things that stand out the most from the four items above and use them to create a sentence. Here's the template:

I use my unique (*include your top unique skills and traits from item 1*) in order to create (*insert the value you add and the best parts of your perfect world vision from item 2*). I will impact (*your group or number of people from item 3*) by (*list the activities that make you happy and excited from item 4*).

Note that your personal mission statement is not bound by time. Think of your mission statement as clarification for the legacy you want to leave.

"Money cannot buy happiness. If you determine what you love to do and follow your passion, the money will come. If you are passionate about something and you dedicate your life to the pursuit of your passion, it will become your purpose and your driving force...Live your life with passion and you will be rich beyond dollars and cents."
~Doug Sandler, Nice Guys Finish First~

Exercise – Define Your Mission

Grab your notebook and write down your mission statement. Here's an example to get you started:

"I use my unique ambition, motivational style, and success to create a business that will help people who want to achieve something big in life and create their own legacy. I will impact 1.3 million people by writing, speaking, and engaging in meaningful relationships."

Baseline

Now that you've penned a rough idea of where you want to go, let's take a moment to figure out where you are today. Some of us are currently very successful yet are always looking to go further. Others of us will have some serious trouble areas we need to work on before we can mentally work on progressing. Regardless of where you are today, this exercise will serve as a way to determine which areas need the most attention and will also help you keep your efforts in balance.

So get started and be honest. This exercise should give you a true idea of your strengths, weaknesses, and desires. It will trigger introspection and ideally give you some strong motivation to blast through this book and apply its principles.

If you've read *Leave the Grind Behind,* you'll be familiar with these questions. But even if you've answered them before, I recommend going through them again. Your score will change over time, and this task is also designed to trigger reflective thinking, which can produce different results day to day.

Alright, let's determine a baseline for your life. And by the way, you can also visit *justingesso.com/quiz* to work through this electronically and be automatically scored.

Exercise – Baseline

For each question, choose the answer that most closely matches your current situation.

Question 1

How do you feel about your income?

- My income is problematic and will not allow me to achieve my goals. I do not track expenses, budget, or plan my earnings. I live week-to-week and struggle to keep up financially.
- I have a standard W-2 job and earn a fair income.
- I budget and have financial goals. I understand variable and passive income and am actively working on adding income streams. I have more than one income stream, but the majority of my pay comes from a standard W-2 job. I can probably have a house with a white picket fence and still have enough saved for retirement, but my goals are much bigger than ordinary. I discuss my income with a group of trusted friends.
- I am making significantly more than I did last year and am on track to make significantly more next year. I am able to make my money work for me. 30% or more of my income comes from passive sources, such as royalties or rents. I am poised to potentially earn large lump sums of money if business plans work out.

- I earn income from 10 or more sources, most of which generate variable pay. Passive income makes up 80% or more of my total income. I budget. I track my income on a weekly basis. I use my income to generate significant monthly cash flow. I earn money from other people's efforts. I have goals for my total income, my number of income sources, and the types of income I earn.

Question 2

How is your net worth performing?

- I don't exactly know my net worth, but I believe I am in debt (I owe more than I own).
- I know my net worth, but it is negative or zero. I have debt, such as cars, student loans, and credit cards. I don't have a precise plan to pay it all off. My debt does not work to build my wealth.
- I track my net worth at least monthly, either by manually graphing it or by using a professional tool. I have a net-worth goal. Still, I'm not exactly proud of my current net worth, and my debt is not working to generate income or business value. I discuss my net worth with trusted friends.
- My net worth is increasing rapidly. I track it in detail and have precise goals and timeline targets. I'm proud of my net worth and am at least in the 80th percentile for my age and location. I have three or more major assets, excluding stocks, contributing to my net worth growth. I don't have any bad debt. Any debt I have is leveraged to increase my wealth and is earning me more than it is costing me.

- I am in at least the 90th percentile and have at least 15 assets, excluding stocks, contributing to significant, rapid portfolio growth. Any debt I have is earning me money.

Question 3

How do you feel about your career?

- I do not enjoy my job. I work for someone else. I come home tired and burned out. I have little energy left to start a new career or develop income on the side. I don't spend enough quality time with my friends and family. I have lost my creative interests and edge. I am deep in the daily grind and don't see a way out.
- I have a standard W-2 job that I enjoy well enough, but I've been in the same job for longer than I had planned. I'm occasionally challenged creatively.
- I enjoy my job and directly impact the company's bottom line. I am regularly challenged creatively. I perform many functions, receive promotions, and change responsibilities regularly. But my efforts go toward achieving my company's goals...not my personal goals. I may have some minor side projects but nothing that will allow me to quit my job.
- I spend 30% of my work time actively achieving my own goals. I am building my own money machines and businesses. I am taking actions to establish my legacy...not someone else's. I am taking charge of my time, but time still feels very limited.
- The only people I work for are customers, largely of my choosing. I have my own businesses and determine how I

will work. I am challenged creatively, work on what I want, and choose when I work. I can work 30 hours or less per week while still achieving my career goals.

Question 4

How is your health?

- I am overweight, do not have a consistent exercise plan, and do not exactly understand which foods I should and shouldn't eat.
- I know which exercises I should do and the types of foods I should eat, but I don't stick to health plans consistently. Perhaps I don't have enough time to work out or prepare healthy meals. Or perhaps I relieve stress with unhealthy habits such as eating sweets or processed foods.
- I have goals for my health, including attaining a low-body-fat percentage, a low heart rate, and a healthy weight. I have identified a long-term reason to make consistently healthy choices today. I regularly read health-related information and understand nutrition. I also understand how to exercise efficiently. However, I am not fully there and need to be more consistent.
- I eat clean foods that promote overall health, longevity, skin tone, anti-aging, and muscularity. I do weight-bearing exercise at least three times per week. I play a sport or otherwise engage in cardiovascular activity at least five times per week. I read a health-related book or magazine at least once per month. I am at an ideal body weight and body-fat percentage. I have healthy vitals and get a physical evaluation at least once per year.

- Being healthy is no longer a day-to-day choice: it is a lifestyle. Processed food makes me feel bad. I completely avoid added sugar. I am highly active and look much younger than my peer group. I achieve success in other areas of my life precisely because of my fitness level.

Question 5

How are your relationships?

- My relationships are struggling. I never have enough time for work and family. I cannot get out of the grind because work and family demands are simply too high. If I don't make immediate corrections, my family and other relationships are in trouble and may result in me losing those I love.

- I find it very difficult to balance my relationships with work and other priorities. I wish I could spend more time with my spouse, children, and/or friends. I do not have a loyal network that I can reach out to for help or ideas. Most of my communication occurs online via email or social media. I find I'm pretty isolated.

- I regularly spend quality time with my family and friends. I do not feel like work and other priorities get in the way of my relationships. My spouse or partner and I are on the same page when it comes to money, career, health, short-term goals, and long-term goals.

- I am actively engaged in the lives of my friends and family. I have habits in place to improve my relationships (attending their events, recognizing their efforts, and listening to them). Each week, I reach out to my network by phone on a rotational basis. I incorporate my family into my success and exercise habits.

- I have a relationship-management tool in place for my contacts, ensuring I recognize birthdays and other major milestones. I have information logged about my network's children, their interests, and other factors that are important to them. Every day, I make personal calls on a rotational basis to at least my top 50 contacts. For my close friends and family, I take time off during standard work hours to participate in their events (attend school lunches, games, go on dates, etc.).

Question 6

How would you rate your creative performance?

- I know which activities I excel at and enjoy. I'm excited and ready to turn those into value that people would pay for, but I don't have a solid plan in place. My skills are a hobby now, but I would love to make a living from them.
- I am actively working on a marketable project that uses my creative strengths. I've created a business plan, tested it, and am in the implementation stage. I will be able to use my creativity in a scalable manner that offers value to many people.
- I am currently making 20% or more of my income from creative pursuits that I enjoy. I have plans in place to expand and spend at least 40% of my work time on these projects. I'm very engaged in my work and excited by it. I wake up ready to get to work.

- 80% or more of my income comes from projects that play off my creative strengths. The passivity of these activities has resulted in me spending 40% or less of my total work time on them. I enjoy my productivity greatly, and it rarely feels like work.

Question 7

Are you active in your community?

- I am not currently involved in any community groups or organizations (business organizations, sports groups, book clubs, church, etc.).
- I am involved in a couple of minor community organizations, but I see people there who are already in my network, such as friends and family. I am not really expanding my network or contributing to a greater cause.
- I am involved with a community group. We meet a couple of times per month, and I enjoy the relationships I'm establishing.
- My community group has a large membership of 50+. We perform charitable work. I am developing deep, lasting relationships that span my personal and business life.
- I am involved in several community groups and hold leadership positions in those groups. I take tremendous satisfaction from my involvement and have built a significant network. I give more than I receive from the community, but I also know the community will help me greatly in any of my ventures. I've earned trust from and developed a personal brand within the organization.

Question 8

How satisfied are you with your life?

- I am not currently happy and don't believe I can significantly change my life. I am stuck.
- I am happy some of the time. I have glimpses of a much better future, but it's easy for me to slip back into old routines, and I fail to make real change in my life.
- I don't love my current situation, but I'm generally pretty happy. I feel positive that I can make real changes in the future.
- I am generally very happy with my life and regularly achieve my goals. I have an excellent outlook on the future. I have made big changes over the last year.
- I am extremely happy. I am achieving big, ambitious goals regularly. I'm genuinely excited about the future. My love of life spills over to—and generates excitement in—those around me.

Capturing your baseline

Before moving on, be sure to jot down any reflective thoughts this quiz triggered. Perhaps you are weaker in a particular area than you expected. Perhaps a great opportunity or idea popped into your mind. Additionally, if you took the quiz online, note your score and the date.

Values

You've now committed to taking the necessary action needed to improve your life. You also have a mission statement that serves as the high-level compass for your actions. You have a baseline measurement for your current situation. Next up are values. Understanding your unique values will help you set and achieve goals in a manner that aligns with your personal beliefs and principles.

Values are completely overlooked in most success programs and business books, but understanding them is critical to your success. First, values help put boundaries on how you will achieve your goals. Second, values help you overcome unsupportive beliefs.

Personally, I value spending time with my family. Before I set out to be independently successful, I assumed that to make a lot of money, I would need to travel frequently and work long hours. This didn't align with my values and unnecessarily prevented me from starting my own businesses sooner. Eventually, I realized I was in charge of my life and could control it by setting a huge income goal while also refusing to sacrifice my family time value.

Once I acknowledged that value, I looked for mentors that were achieving similar goals while also maintaining similar values. The world opened up to me, and I am now able to make much more money and also enjoy more family time. But that is just me and one of my values.

In this way, values apply to your perception of certain goals. Perhaps you believe people who make a lot of money are selfish. What's holding you back from having charitable values? Do you want to climb the ladder without stepping on anyone else? That's a value too.

Or maybe you have no interest in pursuing typical relationships: you want to build an enterprise with 100% focus and zero distraction. You have a singular goal of creating a successful business and value complete commitment to that goal. This is a personal value, and you should not feel badly or judged.

Trying to build a business and your life without understanding your values will lead to friction, and friction will invariably cause failure. You need to understand your personal values and embrace them. Be honest with yourself. You define and accept the value boundaries that you'll operate within. By clarifying your boundaries now, you can build a plan that actually works for you.

 ## Exercise – Determine Your Values

Now, it's time to define some values. Create a list of 10 or more values that will govern your ideal life. What won't you sacrifice (time with family, personal beliefs, free time) while pursuing your goals? What is fundamentally important in your life? Define your behavioral code. Grab your notebook and list your values.

CHAPTER 3

Success Framework

Goals

- Establish habits that will lead to compounding results in life and your business.
- Discover how to stick to successful, constructive behaviors.
- Lock in the habit of making hand-written, daily to-do lists.
- Create between 30 and 100 goals for your life.
- Get specific about how you want your life to unfold.
- Select your top three goals for this year.
- **Action:** Use the daily and monthly worksheets at *justingesso.com/52x.*

Habits

If you save a little money every day, you will soon have a surprisingly large balance in the bank. When you save over many years, the results are almost unbelievable. This, of course, is the magic of compound interest. Similarly, if you take action on a daily basis, the results will compound in your life, delivering unbelievable results. If you work every day toward your goals—

even a little bit—I can guarantee you'll be somewhere completely different this time next year.

> "You will never change your life until you change something you do daily. The secret of your success is found in your daily routine."
> ~Darren Hardy, The Compound Effect~

But there's a problem, and it involves our very nature as human beings. My dog thrives on habit and routine. Any disruption in his routines throws him into a tizzy. He likes dinner at a certain time. He likes to go to bed at the same time and lies in the same place. I can count on him to get antsy in the minutes leading to a precise walk time. He seems happiest sticking to habits and routines.

But I'm not a dog. And neither are you. Habits can become routine, and routine becomes boring. This is especially true of creative types and action takers. We need excitement and novelty. We're here to mix it up and do something big; you and I are not the type to get stuck in a boring routine.

> "When you make poor decisions and do not follow through on obligations and/or key initiatives, you will eventually become known as a person who lacks self-discipline. If this is done for long enough, this type of behavior can have devastating implications for your reputation and brand."
> ~Coyte G. Cooper, Impressions~

Habits are critically important but hard to stick with. Like everyone else, I am guilty of starting great new habits that I know will benefit me tremendously. But before they get locked in, I abandon them. Fortunately, I've learned quite a bit about getting over the hump and actually sticking to the day-to-day actions that change my life. I don't think about eating well, working out, or writing down my goals and to-dos. These things have simply become part of my life. Here are some steps you can take to do so yourself:

Come up with 4-5 new habits today.

Start some life-improvement habits today, addressing areas such as income, health, relationships, and creativity. These can be simple. For relationships, you could compliment your spouse every day. For health, you could work out for 30 minutes each day. For income, you could read one article per day on generating money on your own. For creativity, you can try listening to a meditation three times per week.

Gamify your habit tracking.

Ultimately, habits will become ingrained in your life and will no longer take conscious thought. But when you start new habits, you will need to track their completion. What you track gets results. Why not have fun with this? Seek out an easy, rewarding way to track your progress. Consider apps such as LifeRPG, Habitica, or HabitBull. A simple weekly paper checklist works great too.

Stay motivated by listening to audio books.

You will inevitably lose some motivation (we all do), but don't derail your entire year if you fall into a minor slump. One of the best ways to stay motivated and on track long term is to use your commute and drive time to listen to motivational audio books. Either check out audiobooks from your library (my library has CDs as well as a streaming app) or consider a membership to *Audible.com.*

Listen to highly successful people discuss how they get the most from life. If I ever find myself losing motivation, all I need to do is listen to a great audio book to get right back on track. You'll find almost every successful person talks about the power of habits. Constantly hearing this messaging will have you rolling new success habits into the core of your behavior at record pace.

Mix it up!

Apply what you hear in the audio books. If you have a habit of eating healthy, make sure to change the types of foods you eat. Vary your workouts. Read about income from different sources. Add variability and pull inspiration from wherever you can. Keep it interesting. Remember—you're a human...not a dog.

As you move forward in this book, you'll find more on the types of habits you'll need to successfully start your own business. For now, let's focus on improving your broader life.

 ## *Exercise* – Learn to Love Habits

Grab your notebook and list some new habits. Keep these simple to merely get into the swing of forming great habits.

> "The best thing about the future is that it comes one day
> at a time."
> ~Abraham Lincoln~

Here are some suggestions:

- Create a simple daily habit to improve your income
- Create a simple daily habit to improve your health
- Create a simple daily habit to improve your relationships
- Create a simple daily habit to improve your creativity and how you use it

To-Do Lists

Each day, before logging in to my computer, I write down what I want to accomplish that day. My goal is to write out the items that, if accomplished, would ensure a productive day. This is such a small habit but truly feels like the backbone of my success routine.

> "The very act of working from a list will increase your
> productivity by 25-50 percent the very first day."
> ~Brian Tracy, Get Smart!~

What's most shocking about making a handwritten list is that I usually finish the tasks on my list much faster than I expect, and I certainly accomplish more than if I hadn't written a list. Think about that: I do more in less time.

Often, I'm done by lunch. In other words, I write out a big, daunting list in the morning. I know if I accomplish those items,

I'll feel great about my productivity. I expect the list to take me a full day. Instead, I finish with half my day left. Awesome.

Having completed my list, I can move on to other activities and time segments. I can switch to working on creative big-picture items precisely because my brain isn't cluttered with outstanding things to do. This is particularly great if you're feeling stressed, overwhelmed, or unmotivated. Once you begin to see this process in action, you'll realize how much time you waste if you are unfocused. It's absolutely incredible.

And by the way—I am not an organized person by nature. Planning and organizing are difficult for me. If you've also found it difficult to utilize more involved or complex planning systems, a basic "pen and paper" daily to-do list may be just what you need. The simplicity works wonders for me.

Just remember...the key is to hand write your list. If I write out my to-dos, I get them done. If I type them, I let the list build up. Do a quick search online—you'll find plenty of others have the same experience. I expect it has something to do with separating yourself from the computer screen ritualistically for this habit. It makes the list writing much more purposeful and focused. Regardless of the reason, use good-old pen and paper for this.

Exercise – Download the 52x Daily Tracker

At justingesso.com/52x, you'll find the *52x Daily Tracker* sheet to download. This sheet is specifically designed to help you with the habits and actions throughout this book. Its key feature is a section in which you'll jot down your daily to-do list. With this download in hand, you can either print it or emulate it in your own notebook.

Goals

By now, you've painted a broad picture of the life you want, committed yourself to getting there, determined your values and boundaries, and implemented daily habits. Now, it's time for the exciting part. I want you to very specifically define exactly where you want to be one year from now.

> **"Don't set your goals too low. If you don't need much, you won't become much."**
> **~Jim Rohn~**

At this point, I want you to set broad life goals. Remember, we want your business to serve your goals, not the other way around. So we need to know what you really want from life. This is your opportunity to create great goals. Big goals. Exciting goals.

Here are some great questions to ask yourself:

- How much money do you want to be making?
- How much do you want to be worth?
- How will you be earning money?
- How will you be engaging your creativity?
- What does your recreation and free time look like?
- How much do you travel?
- What's your ideal relationships?
- How do you engage your family, friends, and community?

Now that you have these broader goals, begin to think about why you want a profitable business. Don't look at the specifics of the business, but do look at what you hope to get out of it. Carve out at least 10 goals that specifically define the life results generated by your business.

- Do you want a certain level of passive income?
- Do you want a certain lifestyle and sense of freedom?
- If you have a job now, will you leave it behind?
- Do you want to create a legacy?

Exercise – Set 30+ Goals

With these questions in mind, get out your notebook and write down no fewer than 30 goals. That will get you started. But, since I aim big, strive for 100. I know that feels like a stretch, but writing out 100 goals is an absolutely fantastic exercise. As you write, follow these steps:

Think big. Then, think bigger and sooner.

Put a deadline on each goal and, ideally, a number or something specific and tangible. For instance, don't write "I want to make a lot more money." Instead, write "I want to make $500,000 or more this year." Define your goal so a third party can objectively determine if you've achieved it.

Now, make your goal bigger: make it something for which you'll have to really stretch. If your goals aren't big enough, they won't require you to make the changes necessary to get different results in your life. Big goals are usually no harder to achieve than moderate goals. This is something I never believed until I experienced it myself. Just ensure your goal is big enough to get you out of your comfort zone.

Add emotion to each goal.

If you don't have clear emotions tied to your goals, you're missing a key motivator. Emotions provide fuel. They give us a reason. How will you feel when you accomplish your goal? If your goal is to work out and weigh 180 pounds by the end of the year, is there an emotional element? No! If you want to work out and weigh 180 pounds by the end of the year so you can love playing hard with your kids and ensure you're physically able to travel across the globe with your beautiful wife when you retire, that's a goal with emotional edge!

Emotion adds passion. When you say to yourself *age will not be a factor in my life...I will be younger every year!* you're adding a real, emotional reason to make healthy choices every day.

Put goals in the present tense.

Goals should always be written as if you've already achieved them. In *Psycho Cybernetics*, Dr. Maxwell Maltz does an incredible job of describing how our brains function to achieve goals we set. This goal-seeking mechanism, though, is easy to misuse and is fairly literal. Telling yourself that you want to be a millionaire will cause you to seek the *wanting*. The small tweak of telling yourself you *are* a millionaire will orient your creative powers and actions accordingly.

Put pen to paper.

Don't complicate this. Write down at least 30 goals (and ideally up to 100). Set goals for broader categories (such as health, income, net worth, relationships, career, creativity, and community) and also for what your business will give you. Make them big, measurable, positively worded, and emotionally fueled.

Here's an example: *I have a net worth of $1.8 million or more by December 31st. As a result, I feel excited, fulfilled, and beyond proud. My family is happy and secure, and we're poised to live the life we want...without compromise.*

Now it's your turn.

I encourage you to strive for 100 life goals, but make sure to establish at least 30. You may have no idea how you'll achieve these goals, but that's fine. Define what you want to achieve, and I'll help you get there.

Top Three Goals

You just made a huge list of goals. Now it's time to pick the three that will make the biggest difference in your life. These will become your "Grinder-3 Goals." You will focus on them each and every week going forward. It's likely that, since you picked up this book, at least one of these goals will be to start a profitable business this year. Let's do it!

> "People are not lazy. They simply have impotent goals -
> that is, goals that do not inspire them."
> ~Tony Robbins~

Your Grinder-3 Goals are the goals that will transform your life. You will become obsessed with them. You will work on them five days per week. You *must* get these done *this year*. This is 52x at work. Do today what matters one year from now.

Why do I specifically recommend three goals? Humans have a hard time chasing down multiple efforts at the same time. Whereas trying to do 10 things at once can result in zero things accomplished, working hard on three things is likely to get three things accomplished. As any one of the three is checked off, you replace it and quickly find you've blown 10 total goals out of the water much faster than expected.

I'm not sure if there is a scientific basis for picking three main focus areas, but it's a recommendation and practice I consistently see with big achievers. It also works great for me personally.

 ## *Exercise – Grinder-3 Goals*

Out of your bigger list, choose your Grinder-3 Goals, and write them down in your notebook. These are the goals you want to happen more than anything else. The timeline to achieve these three goals can be anywhere from this month to one year.

Take your time, and refine these goals to ensure they're very specific. Ensure these three goals have the proper elements:

- Do they have a specific deadline or date?
- Will you know precisely when they are achieved?

- Do you have a compelling emotional reason to complete them?
- Are they written in the present tense?
- Do they scare you a little, and will they push you way out of your comfort zone?

If you can answer "yes" to these questions, great! You've done it right. Let's make your goals happen!

Once you have your goals selected, list out any new habits that will help you achieve your Grinder-3 Goals. Finally, use the top three lines of your *Daily Tracker* (at justingesso.com/52x) to outline actions that will help you directly tackle your Grinder-3 Goals.

CHAPTER 4

Your Master Plan

Goals

- Create your vision for the next one, three, five, and 10 years
- Identify what is holding you back from getting the life you want
- Ensure you have the right tasks and habits in place to achieve your vision
- **Action:** Use the daily and monthly worksheets at *justingesso.com/52x*
- **Action:** Take at least one big daily action toward each of your Grinder-3 Goals

Personal Master Plan

You should now have specific and large goals you want to accomplish this year. You should also have a bigger-picture mission statement that is designed to guide your decisions and actions. Let's dial this all in more precisely and lay out where you want to be in the next one, three, five, and 10 years. Again, we are working to design your life plan *before* your business plan.

> **"Anyone can do it. Not everyone will. Will you?"**
>
> **~Gary Keller, The Millionaire Real Estate Investor~**

Some people will complete this exercise in isolation, but generally, you must involve your significant other. This is an enjoyable exercise, and as you both work to paint a picture of your ideal future together, you'll find yourselves bonding even more. During this time, I also want you go back and reference your Mission Statement, your Grinder-3 Goals, and your other brainstormed goals.

 ## *Exercise* – Your Personal Master Plan

For this exercise, I want you to detail where you want to be at certain points down the road. You'll describe who you want to be and what you want to be doing. Following are the questions you should consider and answer:

- Where do you live?
- With whom do you spend your personal and professional time? What is your family and friend situation?
- How do you earn your money? How much money do you earn?
- What is your net worth?
- What physical shape are you in? What is your diet and exercise routine?
- With what community groups are you be involved?
- How do you achieve your mission statement?
- How are you deriving happiness?

You will answer these from the perspective of where you'll be one, three, five, and 10 years from now. Your statements will begin like this:

- In 2018 (or one year from now), *this is how my life looks…*
- In 2020 (or three years from now), *this is how my life looks…*
- In 2022 (or five years from now), *this is how my life looks…*
- In 2027 (or 10 years from now), *this is how my life looks…*

Here's an example:

In 2018, this is how my life looks. I live in a beautiful, modern home in the foothills. I spend my personal time with my wife and children. We are fortunate to have a close-knit set of neighbors—a true community. I earn a steady base of income through passive sources I've established. I also earn surges of money through commissions generated from my business. Etc.

In 2021, this is how my life looks. We live in the same neighborhood and home, but I've doubled down on my engagement in the community by driving local improvement efforts. This has allowed me to gain a strong sense of worth and fulfilment while also expanding my network to include interesting and influential people. I've been afforded this time because my business has management and largely runs itself. I provide oversight and direction but am mostly out of the day-to-day activities. Etc.

In 2022 etc.

You get the idea. The longer and more detailed your vision of the future is, the better. When I do this exercise, I fill up multiple pages in my notebook. So feel free to go off script and into more detail wherever you can. One of the best parts of this exercise happens years later. At some point in the future, you will find your notebook, open it up, and read what you have written. I am continuously amazed by how closely my life has ended up mirroring my writing.

Friction

Now that you've outlined where you want to go, it's time to figure out why you're not there already. What is holding you back from achieving exactly what you want in life?

> "Confront old conditioning. It leads to unconscious behavior....Examine your core beliefs. Hold them up to the light and discard beliefs that make you stuck. ... Your brain must become your ally. If it does not, it will remain your adversary"
> ~Deepak Chopra, MD, and Rudolph Tanzi, PhD, Super Brain~

The mission and goals you have established as part of this program are probably not completely new to you. You may have had these ambitions for years but haven't done anything with them. Perhaps these exercises have caused you to explore new goals or set bigger goals, but fundamentally, you started this book because you already wanted to do something big.

So why have you not already achieved your goals? Why haven't you started your own business already? What's keeping you from getting to that next mile marker? What is holding you back? What's your friction?

 ## *Exercise* – Identifying Friction

In this exercise, I'd like you to be really introspective and honest. This one can be a bit painful, but that probably means you're on track. List at least 20 specific items that are causing friction and holding you back. Dig deep. You don't need to share this list with your friends and family, but I highly recommend you ask for input—others often see your blind spots and have better insight into your friction.

Here are some common points of friction:

- Financial obligations, such as mortgage, kids, and student debt
- Little or no emergency savings
- Lack of time due to job, family, hobbies, etc.
- Insufficient energy
- Limited ideas regarding what to create or sell
- Unsupportive spouse or family
- Lack of technical, sales, or marketing knowledge
- Lack of the right connections
- Residing in the wrong location (city, state, or country)
- Belief you're not smart enough
- Belief that only exceptional people can do big things
- Belief that only people who come from big money can do big things
- Belief that massive success comes from luck

- Belief that only other people can make it big

Grab your notebook and list at least 20 things that are holding you back.

Overcoming Friction

It's time to unleash the beast. Your mind's ability to hold you back can be shockingly powerful. Like the elephant chained from birth, you may have no idea you can easily unshackle yourself.

> "If I've learned anything in life, it is that if you believe something is possible, you tend to focus on the constructive means necessary to make that possibility a reality. I've also learned to believe the opposite. If you don't think something is possible, then you will be blinded to the ways it could be done. It's like a self- imposed blind spot."
> ~Gary Keller, co-founder of Keller Williams Realty International - The Millionaire Real Estate Agent~

You're about to start overcoming your limiting beliefs and self-doubt...your points of friction. You'll define how *your* world works. This is a liberating exercise, but it's no walk in the park.

Affirmations are the tool for this job. Affirmations are highly powerful, and when used correctly, key ingredients in your overall recipe for success.

Want some proof that affirmations work? Look no further than the $100 billion U.S. advertising industry. Has your behavior ever been swayed by an advertisement? No doubt. The core tool of advertising is repetitive messaging that drives your behavior to the advertiser's favor. That, my friend, is affirmative power at work.

In this book, I'm not going to fully dive into affirmations. I devote an entire chapter in my book *Leave the Grind Behind* to the topic, and you can also find plenty of resources on my website *justingesso.com*. If I get back into the full detail here, I'll just be repeating myself. Instead, I want to frame it in the context of why affirmations are so critical when you're starting a business.

Here's how affirmations fold into the daily mental exercises I perform:

- **Daily or weekly writing of goals:** This keeps me focused on the big picture so I can overcome short-term hurdles and accomplish huge goals.
- **Daily handwritten to-do list:** This keeps me taking action every single day so I'm constantly moving toward achieving my goals.
- **Daily meditation:** This helps clear the clutter and allows creative connections and ideas to form.
- **Daily review of affirmations:** This helps me overcome doubt and limiting beliefs, which crop up constantly any time I'm truly doing something big.

All of us have a preconception about how the world works, what we are worth, and how we fit in. This preconception drives much of our behavior. Therefore, changing your preconceptions will change both your behavior and your results. After all, your current situation is the sum result of your previous actions, decisions, and beliefs. If you want to change your situation, you need to change your beliefs.

Think about this in terms of your goals. If you're setting goals that seem unbelievable, doesn't it stand to reason you won't achieve them? You'll think they're too big or too hard. Maybe someone else could achieve them...but not you. Proper affirmations make what you didn't think possible achievable.

Examples of affirmations

Affirmations are written as positive, present-tense statements describing how you want the world to work. They are similar to goals but should work in support of your goals rather than as a substitute for them. Affirmations let you hit yourself with an advertising slogan of your own creation. If they're heard and seen enough, your mind will begin to accept these statements as reality, overcoming past beliefs that built up over time through similar conditioning.

Here are some examples:

- I am running an extremely successful business that brings me huge sums of money while also providing high degrees of personal satisfaction and freedom.
- It's easy for me to create a successful business.
- Owning my own businesses will afford me flexible hours and will allow me to spend awesomely high-quality time with friends and family.
- I spend valuable time with both friends and professional connections who make me feel happy and fulfilled.
- I am doing so well financially that I can readily give $250,000 or more to charity each year.
- I am confident and positive that everything will unfold perfectly in my life.

- My life will be filled with abundance, success, and joy.

- I am toned, lean, and feeling fantastic! I am strong, healthy, and always young.

- I am an absolute money magnet, netting $380,000 or more per year through my own business ventures.

- Money comes to me often and easily.

- I am beyond proud to have built a net worth of $2,300,000.

- I am a positive thinker. My mind is filled every day with positive thoughts, creating a beautiful and positive life for me.

Exercise – Friction Gives Way to Affirmations

Alright, it's time for you to write effective affirmations to help you overcome your limiting beliefs and unshackle the beast within. Tackle your points of friction.

In addition to writing affirmations in your notebook, you'll also put them on notecards. Here's why:

- You'll start a new habit of reviewing your affirmations at least once per day. Bonus points for reading them out loud to yourself. Extra points for memorizing them.

- Whenever you're feeling discouraged, down, uninspired, or otherwise need a "pick me up," reviewing your affirmations is a great way to give yourself a mental reset.

This exercise is complex and will require some time to properly nail down. I suggest doing your own research on affirmations to come up with the right statements for you. I would like you to come up with at least 20 affirmations that tackle the following items:

- Your goals: go back and review your Grinder-3 Goals and larger list from the Goals exercise
- Your perception of starting a business
- Your idea of someone who lives the lifestyle you want
- Your points of friction and what's holding you back
- Your successes, failures, and gaps in income, net worth, career, health, relationships, creative, and community
- Your self image: what do you believe about yourself that may be affecting your situation (education, location, genetics, etc...)

Alright, get to it. In your notebook, write out at least 20 different affirmations. Be sure to also hand write these on note cards for easy reference any time.

Stopping Point

If, in your points of friction, you've found something very serious that requires a significant amount of your attention to properly address, you may need to stop reading this book and work with a professional. If we assume you can work on three major goals at any point, but you have a major health issue and a toxic relationship with your spouse, that's two of your three right there. And your third goal will likely be simply to "get by" financially. You frankly won't have room to successfully craft your life through a small business. Once you've worked through those major issues, you'll be ready to come back to this book.

If this is the case, don't take it as a bad sign. Perhaps this is something you've needed to acknowledge and tackle. By focusing your energy directly onto these issues directly, you'll more quickly navigate through them and move onto the next. Just like I and many others had a rude awakening, maybe you're about to also.

If, on the other hand, your friction seems manageable using the tools I've provided here, let's charge forward!

Take Stock

Wow! You've knocked out Part I: Lifestyle Design. This was a heavy set of exercises and introspection. But I hope you see how valuable it is to start with yourself before jumping into a new business.

Before you move on, let's review where we've been and ensure nothing has fallen through the cracks. This short exercise will validate just that. If you answer "not yet" to any of the following questions, pause, go back, and sincerely complete the exercise and put the practice in place. I want you to surrender to this book and let the exercises and habits do their work.

 Exercise – Take stock

Question 1

Have I written down at least three objectives I want this book to help me with? Do I know why I started this book and what I hope to get out of it?

- Yes
- Not yet

Question 2

Do I know my mission statement, and did I write it down on the worksheet from *justingesso.com/52x*?

- Yes
- Not yet

Question 3

Am I finding ways to keep myself motivated and energized? For example, do I listen to audio books whenever I have a chance, particularly during commutes? Do I also understand audiobooks help me think creatively and expand my knowledge? Do I know that if I don't constantly manage my motivation, I likely won't stick to this or any other endeavor?

- Yes
- Not yet

Question 4

Am I actively using a tool, such as Habitica, to gamify and make habit tracking enjoyable? At this point, have I filled this system with habits and tasks such as reading affirmations, writing down goals, and writing out to-do lists?

- Yes
- Not yet

Question 5

Do I hand write my Grinder-3 Goals once per day? Am I excited to achieve them?

- Yes
- Not yet

Question 6

Have I established my one-, three-, five-, and 10-year master plan? Do I know where I want to go in life? While I understand this will evolve over time, do I realize it serves as a strong guidepost for my actions today?

- Yes
- Not yet

Question 7

Do I understand exactly what has been holding me back from achieving the life I want? Have I detailed my points of friction?

- Yes
- Not yet

Question 8

Have I crafted at least 20 affirmations? Have I hand-written them on note cards, and do I review these note cards at least once per day? Do these affirmations directly tackle my points of friction and excite me about achieving my goals?

- Yes
- Not yet

Question 9

Each and every day, am I taking at least one action (to-do) on each of my Grinder-3 Goals? Am I employing 52x thinking by doing today what will matter one year from now?

- Yes
- Not yet

Question 10

Am I taking each section's exercises seriously? Am I spending time on crafting personal and well-thought-out answers? Am I not rushing or short-changing myself? Do I understand the value is there, but only if I give it my all?

- Yes
- Not yet

Question 11

If I'm struggling with ANYTHING in this book, am I avoiding letting that deter me? Do I ask for help, input, and support from my spouse, friends, or network? Will I also not hesitate to email justin@justingesso.com or find another way to get the support I need to move forward and do an awesome job? Do I understand this sort of introspection is challenging and that many of my best ideas will come from interacting with others?

- Yes
- Not yet

And most importantly...

Question 12

Over the course of Part I, have I designed a lifestyle that is so ridiculously compelling that I will do whatever it takes to make it happen? Have we identified that greener grass of yours?

- YES!!!!!
- Not yet...looks like I have some revising to do

Whenever I talk to someone who has effectively left the grind behind, they simply cannot imagine ever going back to a regular job. They've chosen to make themselves unemployable, even if offered the highest salary. Like me, they will do whatever it takes to stay where the grass is greener. I need you to be there too.

Part II

Foundation

Part II Introduction

In Part I, we looked at a more general picture of life success, motivation, and happiness. Part II is going to more specifically dive into *business* success factors. Said another way, let's look at those practices that will enable you to start and run successful businesses.

CHAPTER 5

People

Goals

- Understand the importance of people to your business success
- List your Top 50 network connections
- Establish a system for improving engagement with your connections and tracking your progress
- Get into the routine of developing real relationships
- Establish the habit of contact
- **Action:** Use the daily and monthly worksheets at *justingesso.com/52x*
- **Action:** Take at least one big daily action toward each of your Grinder-3 Goals

Your Top 50

We've all heard the saying, "It's not what you know, but who you know," and if you want to start a successful business, you'll need to live and breathe that saying. Even if you plan to market a product solely to strangers online, don't underestimate the role your people network plays. Proper management of your network is 100% critical.

> "It's not what you know; it's who you know."
> ~Who Knows?~

In fact, if I look at where I am today, it's because of people. It's because of the relationships I've developed. Once I developed the right mindset, all it took was connecting with the right people. People provide support, connections, knowledge, ideas, and so much more. We progress and advance because we learn from those who came before. Your network gives you the ability to level-jump results, avoid pitfalls, and leverage others' connections. This chapter will help you establish the right habits and systems to ensure the people in your network contribute to your success.

In fact, the concepts in this chapter are so important that you'll find entire coaching systems dedicated to them. One of the coaching programs I personally used spent 80% of its weekly focus on managing and dealing with people. It was the most expensive program I have done by a long shot, but it was well worth it.

As I watch businesses succeed and fail—whether through my coaching, consulting, or day-to-day interactions—I can best gauge a company's likelihood of continued success by observing the owner's attention to people. This doesn't mean you need to be a schmoozer or uber-charismatic person (I certainly am not), but it does mean you need to deliberately make and maintain meaningful connections with people.

> "...as most long-term investors will tell you, there's a good chance that the relationships you build today will have a way of coming back to benefit you in the future."
> ~J Scott, The Book on Negotiating Real Estate~

I have a very important message for you...

Be warned: the exercises in this chapter will challenge most everyone. If you fail to stick to anything in this entire book, I expect it will be these exercises. They're not hard, but most people simply won't do them. Consequently, most people won't achieve what they really want from life and won't start a successful business. If you want to be the exception—if you want to be in the minority—you need to really commit yourself to this chapter.

Likewise, if you believe the Internet, email, and social media has replaced traditional forms of engaging with important people, you're in for a rough road.

 ## *Exercise* – List Your Top 50 Contacts

Within your life, you will have a certain subset of people who enable your success. They fuel you with ideas, connect you with the right people, and literally drop opportunities in your lap. You need to identify these people, deliberately improve your relationship with them, and continuously be of service to them.

This exercise is straightforward. I want you to list at least the "Top 50" people in your life. This list should be made up of friends, family, and business people. As you progress, you'll get a better idea of how we'll use this list. For now, simply know that these are people with whom you will meaningfully connect on a regular basis. You will ask about their lives. You will share your message. You will simply build deeper relationships, and as a result, your life will change dramatically.

You can start smaller—perhaps with 20 people—but I'd like you to grow it to your Top 50 over time. If you have more people you want to list, that is fine. But I specifically want you to maintain an exclusive Top 50 group comprised of the 50 most important people in your life.

Alright, grab your notebook and list the names of 20 to 50 important people in your network. These can be friends, family, or business people. The more influential they are, the better. These people will become your champions. And, name the list "Top 50," even if it includes fewer. This will help you remember to aim for 50, regardless of how many you start with. You can have great relationships with these people already, or they can be people you need to get to know better. Nurturing these relationships will be a primary contributor to your success.

Systematize Your Contacts

To this point, we've been very much developing the "business of you." You have a mission statement, goals, and more. You are now sitting comfortably as your life's CEO. As CEO, it's time to act like a business. Great businesses have systems to track their contacts, customers, and prospects. Great businesses understand the tremendous value in managing the people that surround them.

I'm imparting in you the crucial knowledge that your network needs to be one of the single most valuable assets you have. Just like you'd track anything else important in your life, like money, you need to track people. If you want deeper relationships, you need a system to help you manage relationships effectively.

Let's start systematizing your contacts. Grab your Top 50 people list, and let's enter them into a contact-management tool. This tool needs to be something that can store names, email addresses, phone numbers, mailing addresses, birthdays, and general notes.

For many companies, Salesforce is the go-to option for this job. However, that's probably overblown for your situation. Most of us can simply use Google Contacts or Outlook to record this information. Ideally, your tool will sync contact dates to your calendar, giving you reminders for birthdays and other significant milestones. I personally use HubSpot.com, which is a free tool similar to Salesforce.

Whichever tool you pick, make sure it's easy and functional. Make sure it's something you'll actually use. It should also be accessible, ideally syncing to your computer and phone, making your contacts available to you anywhere. And keep it simple: technology should be an enabler, not a roadblock.

 ## *Exercise* – Systematize Your Contacts

To complete this exercise, choose a tool and enter your contacts. Enter as much data about each contact as you can, such as:

- Name.
- Phone.
- Email.
- Mailing Address.

- Birthday.
- Spouse's Name.
- Kids' Names.
- Important Dates.
- Favorite Sports.
- Favorite Foods.
- Interests/Ambitions.
- Notes from prior conversations.
- Top 50? (Yes/No)

Now, consider these questions:

- Am I committed to using this tool and updating it on a weekly basis?
- Will I record information about my contacts so I don't have to worry about remembering everything?
- Do I understand that, by having information about my contacts, I'm demonstrating that I value them as individuals?

Work Your Contacts

Now that we've identified and captured your contacts, it's time to figure out what to do with them. This is very tactical and requires you to work your contact list every week. This simply must become a habit. Most people will find themselves resisting this task; however, it will eventually become second nature. By the time you're ready to launch your business, this habit must already be in place, and your business will then have the people support it needs. If you establish this habit now, trust me, you'll thank yourself when it comes time to launch your business.

> "You'll find that when you share your vision, some people will want to help you make it happen. Others will introduce you to friends and resources that can help you. You'll also find that each time that you share your vision, it becomes clearer and feels more real and attainable. And most importantly, every time you share your vision, you strengthen your own subconscious belief that you can achieve it."
> ~Jack Canfield, The Success Principles~

As I said earlier in this chapter, most people will fail to commit to this exercise. Don't be most people—be the exception...and become exceptional.

One hour on Fridays

Every Friday, I want you to call 10 people from your Top 50 list. Notice that I said *call*. I didn't say use email, Facebook, or Twitter. This exercise is about building meaningful relationships with people. In-person meetings are best, but phone calls are a close second.

What this really means is you need to set aside a one- to two-hour block on Fridays to make these calls. It's not that hard. Does leaving a message count? No. That doesn't really add value. I want you to converse with 10 of your Top 50 people each week.

Salespeople understand the value of this exercise. Successful sales people live and die by the strengths of their relationships. If you're not in sales, this may be new to you. But guess what: you're building your brand and a business—you need to be your own best salesperson.

The value

Apart from building meaningful relationships, which has its own strongly intrinsic rewards, you are also setting up something very important. When it comes time for you to actually sell something, you will have a key group of evangelists who will be excited to hear about what you're up to. They'll tell their friends. They'll become your launch pad.

If you don't put in the time to build these relationships up front, your product launches or offerings won't be fueled by your relationships, and you will flop. Like anyone, as you work toward your dream life, you will get stuck, become overwhelmed, and find yourself challenged. But within your network is someone who will help "clear the path" when you need it most.

And as a last note, asking you to contact ten people by phone each week is nothing! *This is your warmup.* In the expensive coaching program I mentioned earlier, I was on the hook for calling 60 people *every week* (plus meeting at least 10 in person and attending one to two networking events).

It was very hard for me to get into the habits the program required, but once I did, my results completely changed. You'll notice the same change in your results, and I hope you blow 10 calls per week out of the water. If you want to make it big, don't settle for ten calls. Reach for 100. Get it done.

> "Ego driven, insecure individuals can't bear to crack the thin veneer of their egos and won't venture into the unknown. In other words, they won't push the envelope."
> ~John Shufeldt, Ingredients of Outliers~

Alright, what do you say when you call? Keep it simple and ask questions. Here are some examples:

- "Hey, I just thought I'd give you a call to check in. I'm trying to make a more deliberate effort to keep in contact with my network."
- "Hi, it's been awhile since I checked in—I just wanted to see how you're doing."
- "What are you up to this weekend?"
- "What do you think about grabbing a cup of coffee next Tuesday?"
- "I was looking at LinkedIn and noticed you got a promotion!"
- "I saw that picture you posted on Facebook. Hilarious! What happened?"

In short, ask questions and let the conversation flow. Make the call about them. Let the relationship grow over time. Each conversation will get easier. If you have a hard time with this, you can quickly become a pro by reading *How to Win Friends and Influence People* by Dale Carnegie.

 ## *Exercise* – Work Your Contacts

Alright, now it's time for you to take action. Whip out your notebook and hand write these four statements:

- I am committed to calling and talking to at least 10 people every week.
- I am committed to improving and developing my network and understand this will take consistent nurturing.
- I have set up a one-hour block on my calendar as a recurring event every Friday,
- During my hour, I will shut off email and other distractions. I will not slack on this. This is one of the habits that will separate me from the pack. Most people won't do this. I'm not most people.

CHAPTER 6

Money and Time

Goals

- Learn to think differently about how money is made and kept
- Identify how you're truly using your money and time
- Make data-based changes in your approach to money and time
- Eliminate waste and maximize your money and time
- **Action:** Use the daily and monthly worksheets at *justingesso.com/52x*
- **Action:** Take at least one big daily action toward each of your Grinder-3 Goals

The Two Big Excuses

When it comes to weaseling out of accomplishing what people want from life, no two excuses come up more often than time and money. Since I want you to start profitable businesses, I wrote this chapter to strip away those excuses. But be prepared for unique approaches to this problem. Rather than focusing on expenses, we'll focus on income. Rather than just talking about time suckers, we're going to actually track and analyze your day-to-day life.

Remember, there are people out there right now accomplishing massive goals. You can readily find people who run multiple successful businesses, have a rich personal life, and publish multiple high-quality books every year. These people know how to optimize and leverage their money and time. This chapter's exercise is a challenge, but it is well worth it. This is your chance to eliminate time and money from your plate of excuses.

Money Primer

Nearly all of us have been conditioned and educated in a manner that doesn't support the sort of lifestyle we want. We are taught to work hard to achieve mediocre money results. T. Harv Eker said it best when it comes to the way we're conditioned:

> "Rich people have their money work hard for them. Poor people work hard for their money."
> ~T. Harv Eker, Secrets of the Millionaire Mind~

While that quote looks at rich versus poor, I see the difference in owner versus worker as well. Business owners tend to have very different approaches to earning money. Let's dive into the unique ways most business owners think about money.

Change Your conditioning

If you want to learn how to really make money, don't expect your traditional education to have the answers. In fact, throughout my entire formal education, the process of making money was never really explored.

Traditional education teaches you to be a Cog...a worker. Grinder education teaches you that making real money is a game that you can control. In fact, if you're passionate about the money *game*, opportunities will open everywhere, and you will thrive.

I just said school doesn't teach you how to make money, but I'm going to take it a step further: it actually conditions us all wrong. We are conditioned to realize mediocre financial results. We are explicitly conditioned against being a Grinder and owner. We are conditioned to think: *It takes too much money; I'll need startup capital and big loans; I'll have months where I lose money; it's just too risky; I could lose everything; success is an exception; it's big corporations or nothing.*

With beliefs and limiting statements like these, how does anyone become successful? It's time for a change. It's time to start thinking about how real money is made and held. It's time to enable yourself through reconditioning.

So how does a Grinder think? Grinders think about two key metrics: net worth and scalability. Net worth gives us our big-picture, long-term view. Scalability gives us strategic direction in our day-to-day actions.

The big picture: net worth...your balance sheet

Thinking about net worth first—rather than specific account balances, monthly income, and monthly expenses—is something that you'll need to begin doing.

Why? Net worth compels you to focus on long-term goals and removes the day-to-day noise. Eliminating the day-to-day noise is a must for business owners. Your income will undoubtedly swing wildly from month-to-month, or even week to week. I've seen more than my share of people who fail simply because their spending follows their erratic earning. Even though they may earn more than me, their manic spending during upswings is always paired with trouble during downswings. When it comes to money, they are looking at the day-to-day details, not the big picture.

To get out of this destructive cycle, start thinking about net worth, which forces your mind to focus on the big moves you can make that will impact your overall wealth. Rather than spending money on items that lose value, you spend money on items that generate income and can be reasonably expected to grow and appreciate.

Net worth also forces you to think big. This is where you make big plays. If you look at your day-to-day income, you might feel earning an extra $1,000 per month sounds pretty great. But, if you zoom out to the net worth level, does an extra $1,000 per month really move the needle?

This thought pattern is another factor that helped me quit my corporate job with confidence. At the time, most people earned 3% raises each year. Top performers possibly received 5%, 7%, or maybe even more. Those numbers seemed fine at first glance, but as soon as I switched my thinking to net worth and projected out those raises, I realized I wasn't going to see significant growth any time soon. I needed a faster path.

Another term for net worth is *balance sheet*. Throughout this book, you've begun implementing successful business best practices into your personal life. Here's the chance to do that for your personal money. Start making balance-sheet oriented decisions about your finances. These are the types of questions to ask yourself as you think about money:

- Will this purchase help me generate income?
- Will the value of this purchased item likely increase?
- Will this career or business decision make a real difference on my balance sheet, or will it be unnoticeable?
- If I get this loan, can I use it to generate money or buy something that will increase in value? How can I get debt to pay for itself and then some?
- If I leverage my money more (e.g. use less cash to buy a rental property), can I stay cash-flow positive *and* build my balance sheet faster?

You may have noticed these questions force you to view decisions through a net-worth lens, which highlights the usefulness of good debt. Indeed, every major jump in my net worth originated as a debt. This doesn't mean I financed a new car (an asset that loses value and generates no income). This means as soon as you have a great idea that is capable of generating money, you take it on and multiply your results using other people's money (debt). Using debt to improve your balance sheet allows you to remove personal financial limitations and achieve much larger results.

Scalability and your profit-and-loss sheet

If you achieve a breakthrough in results, do you also receive a breakthrough in pay? The answer to that question quickly reveals if you're a worker or an owner...a Cog or a Grinder. It's the question you should ask yourself with every new opportunity and idea.

Think about our most limited resource: it's time....not money. Therefore, if you bind your income to time, you will artificially limit your income. If you earn a salary, you limit your earnings. Scalability is all about getting into the mindset that income should *not* be attached to time. Scalability involves putting in approximately the same amount of effort, whether you sell 10 or 10,000 units of something. Scalability allows you to earn $1,000 or $1,000,000 with equal ease.

Scalability focuses your attention on your *profit-and-loss statement*, the companion to your balance sheet. This is simply your income compared to your expenses. But let me stress: this is a secondary concern. Despite what you read in countless personal finance books, the majority of your decisions should not be made at this level. Saving $2 per day by skipping Starbucks is fine, but that decision will not make you a millionaire. Perhaps if you divert enough penny-pinching decisions into an investment account, you could become a millionaire by the time you're ready to retire, but I don't want to wait that long.

Here's the winning approach I consistently see:

- Keep your personal expenses in check, but don't spend too much time concerning yourself with expenses. Conduct something like a quarterly expense audit to ensure you're not needlessly wasting money.
- Find a way to earn just enough money in a steady manner to cover your basic living expenses. We'll talk about this more later, but this should be reasonably steady business income. Most businesses typically have one long-term

client that covers this base set of expenses. The goal here is to alleviate stress and short-term thinking. This income should consume a small percentage of your business time (say 20%). Alternatively, perhaps your spouse's income covers this for your family.

- Spend the remaining 80% of your time working on generating scalable income sources—ideas that can be expected to be visible on your balance sheet.

Holding your feet to the fire

There is one last principle I want to discuss.

Changing your money orientation from *I'll just stop buying Starbucks* to *I'll buy income-producing real estate* is a scary prospect for almost everyone—so much so that they never do it, even though the money is available to help you. But something interesting happens to me every time I make a big, scary purchase: it holds my feet to the fire, and as a result, I up my game.

> "Are you reading a list of "10 Steps to Quit Your Job?" Just skip ahead to step ten."
> ~Brandon Virgallito~

It's one thing to write down your goals, but it's another thing to put yourself in a situation that requires you to find a way to perform. Here are two examples from my personal life.

When I decided to quit my job, I also decided to move out of our house. A good application of the principles in this chapter would be to buy and move into a duplex and rent out half. This would have provided security while I found my way in the noncorporate world. It would have then parlayed well into a solid rental property once I was ready to move up. But my wife wasn't having it. Quitting my job and moving away from our families was bad enough. So instead, we decided to move to a much nicer—and more expensive—house. It was in a fast-growing market, and I got a good deal, so I expected it to be positive on my balance sheet but rough on my profit-and-loss numbers.

This situation turned out much better than expected, and to this day, I am thankful for my wife's insistence on doing it. Increasing my housing expense pushed me way out of my comfort zone. I was forced to perform. I was forced to make big decisions rather than small ones. I might still be in a duplex making mediocre decisions because my feet wouldn't have been held to the fire.

Similarly, in the opening of this book, I mentioned I recently purchased a Tesla Model S. A new-car purchase goes against every principle in this chapter. But, it holds my feet to the fire. That's the only way I can justify it. It is not good for my balance sheet. It is not good for my profit-and-loss numbers. It does, however, force me to once again up my game and live up to a higher standard.

I suppose for every rule there is an exception. I hope you follow the money rules in this chapter 90% of the time. And if you do break them, I'll give you a pass as long as they hold your feet to the fire.

Exercise – Start Tracking Your Money

We are going to dive deeper into the business side of money, but starting today, let's track your personal finances like a business. Tracking your financial data in the construct described in this chapter will force your orientation, goals, and actions to shift in the right direction.

Use the *52x Money Master Worksheet* at https://justingesso.com/52x. Here's how:

- Fill out this worksheet once per month…starting this week.
- Put your business (tax-related) expenses in Section A. You may not have any yet.
- Include your income in Section B.
- Calculate your monthly taxable income in Section C.
- Put big-picture info, such as your net worth, in Section D.

Time Primer

If you're anything like me, time is a problem! How do you start successful businesses on the side or as full-time endeavors when your life is already full? Fortunately, there are highly effective methods for optimizing your use of time. After all, the biggest achievers in history had the same time constraints as you and me. It's just a matter of how you use it.

> **"The essence of self-discipline is to do the important thing rather than the urgent thing."**
> **~Barry Werner~**

Some motivation before you start

I spent a lot of my corporate career implementing time- and money-saving processes for various organizations. I applied specific methodologies, tools, and statistics to identify and eliminate huge amounts of unseen waste. When I decided to leave the corporate world, I realized I could apply the same methodologies, tools, and analyses to my own life.

This exercise became instrumental to quitting my corporate job. To achieve my goals, I knew I needed more time and more money. I had a full-time job, a young child, a wife, and every excuse in the world to be *too busy* to accomplish what I really wanted. Once I completed exercises to track my time and money and then made the right changes, I ended up saving $741 per month and three hours per day (that's $8,800 and 1,008 hours per year, respectively). That was gold...and all I needed to make the jump. You can read more about the specifics in my book *Leave the Grind Behind*.

Since leaving my six-figure corporate job, I continue to revisit this exercise. I currently do what most people would probably consider about three to four full-time jobs, yet I don't work long hours. In fact, I "work" much less than when I had my corporate job and feel I have a very balanced life. So, let's just say I know a thing or two about optimizing time.

Finding time is critical

As you know, our daily actions and habits compound into big results. Time is no different. Time comes down to our day-to-day choices. If you are ruthless about your time, you will make time. And if you are going after a goal that is truly in line with your passions, you will want to devote your time and energy to it.

To help, you will need to gather data on your actual behavior. Data is objective, but your brain is not. So to do this right, we need to collect information about how you're actually spending time in your day. If you haven't tracked areas of your life or job before, this may seem unnatural, but give it a couple of weeks, and I think you'll be surprised.

Once you've collected the data, you'll then assign dollar values to your time. Even if you earn a flat fee, this is important because it will demonstrate how your earned-income rate increases if you become more efficient—especially once you run your own business. It will also help direct you toward work areas you should be spending more time on.

What if you work a regular job?

If you work in a job that completely dictates your time, such as a call center, you still need to do this exercise. And separating your "Value Add" and "Non-Value Add" work time (more on this below) is still very valuable. When you get to the analysis, you'll see how this plays out and how you can use it to your advantage.

The principles in this chapter apply no matter your job type. The actions you take may vary, but the principles won't.

Exercise – Start Optimizing Your Time

For the next two weeks, utilize the *52x Time and Income Optimizer* at justingesso.com/52x. Make sure you understand it. If you have any questions, reach out to me at justin@justingesso.com.

You'll find the full instructions along with the optimizer, but let me set the stage here. We are going to begin classifying your time into "value add" and "non-value add" segments. The exercise will also layer in how "focused" you are on given time segments. We don't want your success to come at the expense of family, health, or any other area of personal importance. This is not what I want for myself or for you. So, assigning value to our use of time is a critical part of this exercise.

As mentioned earlier, this is built on the exact approach I've used to help save companies millions of dollars. I revisit this exercise regularly in my life. And for the people I coach, it often churns out the most fascinating insights and biggest revelations of any exercise we do.

It does require that you get detailed and track your activities for two weeks. There is a commitment required from you, but once you begin to see the value of the information unfold, I'm 100% confident this will be a life-changing exercise.

Important insights await! Get started with your tracking.

Time and Income

Once you've begun tracking your time in the *52x Time and Income Optimizer*, you will go back and overlay your income data. This will give you insight into how your money is actually earned, what your current potential is, and where you should direct more of your energy.

This exercise is a fascinating way to baseline where you are today. But as you begin layering in more and more income streams, you will want to revisit this on a regular basis.

This exercise explores several concepts that illustrate how you can best leverage your time for money. As before, even if you simply work a nine-to-five job that pays a fixed rate, it's still important for you to track your time. This will give you insight into your true value and ways you can improve your situation.

Exercise – Complete Two Weeks of Time & Money Tracking

Whereas time needs to be tracked as it happens, money data can be input after the fact. Once you've tracked some time data, go back and overlay the money data. Complete at least two weeks of tracking before you dive into the analysis.

You'll find full instructions for doing this properly in the *52x Time and Income Optimizer* at justingesso.com/52x.

Money and Time Analysis

Alright, once you've collected two weeks of data, we're going to wrap up, analyze, and then create significant actions you can take. This has the power to completely overhaul your time and money situation...removing them as barriers and concerns.

And in case you find this tracking hard or challenging:

> **"If you are willing to do only what's easy, life will be hard. But if you are willing to do what's hard, life will be easy."**
>
> **~T. Harv Eker~**

Exercise – Analyze Your Data

We all waste our talent and energy in the form of poorly used time and money. Let the data guide you toward maximized life results. Here's what to look for:

- Average hourly earnings
- Hours worked per day
- Value-add time vs non-value add time
- Focus
- Passive income

What if I work in a standard job and can't control these factors?

Everything you see here applies to your work situation, whether or not you're working for yourself. In fact, I used many of these concepts while at an entry-level call center job. By learning how to be more efficient and productive, you are preparing for the day you run your own gig. But this also translates to awesome performance at your current job. Performing well increases your chances of getting a promotion, earning more money, making better people connections, and building more control and freedom into your day.

Simply put, you will be more efficient and consistent. By following the principles here, you will fast track your career. Without further ado, here are the points of analysis you'll find in the worksheet:

Wasted Time

The *52x Time and Income Optimizer* brings your non-value-add (NVA) time front and center. This is waste. Consider how much non-value-add time you have. How much repetitive mindless work do you do that no one cares about? How much excess TV, gaming, and social media surfing do you partake in? Add this time up in your sheet.

I'm going to assume you are already a motivated person, and that's why you're reading this book. Despite that, you likely spend a much each day on NVA activities. If you have six hours per day of NVA time (looking at both work and home), that's 42 hours per week...or 2,184 hours per year.

The average American now consumes media for about 10.5 hours per day (*Nielsen's Q1 2016 Total Audience Report*). That doesn't even include other types of waste, which when added together, bump wasted-time estimates to somewhere around 15.5 hours per day! If you're the average, that's 108.5 hours per week...or 5,642 hours per year!

What's your number? Be honest with yourself, and write it down.

Focus Factor

What is your average focus rate for the week? Are there certain activities you focus on better than others? Look at your "Focus Dollar Gap" figure. This is how much additional value you have to offer if you did deep work each day.

By looking at the numbers and playing with the "What If" sheet, you can see how detrimental poor focus is. Indeed, by focusing your time, you'll feel as though you're creating time out of nowhere.

Constantly switching back and forth between tasks (such as bouncing between what you're working on, email, phone, social media) is much more impactful than you might realize. Numerous studies have shown the tremendous "switching cost" you pay as your brain switches from task to task, concept to concept, or segment to segment.

In fact, according to the American Psychological Association, switching between activities rather than focusing on one at a time results in a 40% productivity loss (*Who Multi-Tasks and Why? Multi-Tasking Ability, Perceived Multi-Tasking Ability, Impulsivity, and Sensation Seeking by Sanbonmatsu DM, Strayer DL, Medeiros-Ward N, Watson JM*).

This switching cost is a multiplier on whatever focus rate you have. If, during your work hours, your focus rate averages less than 80%, you need to take corrective action.

Passive Income

Hopefully this exercise shows you the insane power of passive income—that is, income you receive without applying direct work effort. We'll dive into passive income in Part III, but suffice to say that you want to do everything in your power to find ways to generate as much of it as possible.

Annualized Potential

This number shows you what you would earn if you were 100% focused during work hours. What's the real potential value you offer your company or customers?

Said another way, it shows the cost of distractions. It puts, in monetary terms, how much allowing distraction into your day harms you. And by the way, this value is understated given the overall drop in productivity that comes from switching between tasks.

Use this number to see the true value you have to offer...and start living up to it!

Maximized Annual Potential

If you focus 100% on only value-add activities for eight hours per day, what sort of income would you generate? This is an important thought exercise and a goal you should strive for.

What-If Scenario

Now that you have an idea of how these numbers all come together, head over to the "What If" sheet on the spreadsheet and play around with the numbers. What if you made more money per hour? What if you had more passive income? What if you focused more but worked less?

Use this to set goals and milestones for yourself. Understand that doing more with your life is readily within your power.

You control time. You control money.

Eliminate Waste

Alright, all of this data, analysis, and critical thinking is leading to this: eliminate waste! It's time to transform your analysis into an action plan.

Using your data, come up with three numeric targets for yourself. This is a data-driven exercise. Find anything that is wasting your energy and talent.

Wasted time is an epidemic. To reiterate the numbers from the last lesson:

- If you're pretty motivated, you likely spend about six hours per day on NVA time, when looking at time spent both at work and at home. That's 42 hours per week...or 2,184 hours per year.

- If you're an average American, you're spending closer to 15.5 hours on wasted time every day. That's 108.5 hours per week...or 5,642 hours per year!

We need to replace that time with doing something productive that you love; something that adds value to your life and the life of those around you; something you'll care about and remember 52 weeks from now.

There are three fundamental actions you can take to eliminate wasted time:

- Stop
- Automate
- Delegate

And again, whether you work for yourself or a company, this information applies to you.

1. Stop

This is by far the easiest and most liberating option. But people have a tough time doing it! Do you send a report to your boss every week that takes you three hours to put together? Does she care about the report? Or, was it something a prior boss put in place, and now you're stuck doing things "the way they've always been done?"

Look for opportunities to stop doing things people don't really care about. Or...do fewer of them. Maybe you need to do that report but once per month is just fine.

There are likely many personal things you can stop doing that will also save you time and money. Perhaps it's time to cancel your TV service or other time sucks that you're paying for.

Will what you're doing now make a difference one year from now? Will you care about it (or even remember it) on your deathbed? Whether professional or personal, we all have many things that we can simply stop doing in order to make way for something more important.

2. Automate

If you are doing non-value-add work that you can't stop, look for automated ways to reduce the amount of time you need to spend on it. A good indicator that automation is the right solution is when you find yourself repeating the same task over and over. If it feels robotic, a robot can do it.

To get some creative juices flowing, here are four common ways you can think about automation:

1. Templates

If you regularly send similar emails, put together email templates. Gmail, Outlook, and other programs support templates. Templates save time and reduce errors, which means you to do your job better and more efficiently.

2. FAQs and great documentation

Do you spend a lot of time answering the same questions? Get those answers documented and made widely available.

3. Systematic automation in big companies

If you work for a company and have identified a repetitive yet automatable task, make sure to let the right people (like your boss) know. Companies have plenty of automation initiatives and love finding ways to save money, but they aren't always aware of the opportunities that exist. Sharing opportunities makes you look good and helps the company. It's not going to eliminate your job. Quite the contrary: it makes you more valuable. Win-win.

There's also a big multiplier here: if many people in your company are doing this repetitive task, you should multiply your time or monetary savings across that number of employees. Often, 15 minutes saved in a daily process can multiply up to millions in savings for companies. This stuff can make you a hero. It's exactly how I made my name and achieved promotions at my companies.

4. Systematic automation in your own company

Manual processes are the slow death knell of small businesses. They result in expensive labor and inconsistent delivery and quality. Ensure you are thinking automation from Day 0 as much as possible.

Often, this means partnering with or hiring someone who can integrate online systems. No longer do companies need dedicated programmers to achieve automation—many online systems can communicate with each other and can be linked. For example, orders from one a website can pass data to your CRM, your shipping company, and your financial tracking software. You just have to set this up. Don't do it manually.

Hiring someone who can do this is much more valuable than hiring people to manually process orders. In fact, you can probably hire a college or high school student to knock this stuff out for you. And when it comes to online systems, many of them will run for small, predictable monthly fees that are much cheaper than manual labor costs to do the same. Take advantage of how accessible systems integration has become, and eliminate manual processes from the start.

3. Delegate

If you can't eliminate or automate, you may be stuck with a necessary non-value-add item that requires a person. The answer for these items is to delegate them.

1. Delegate to a subordinate

This is what most people think of when they think delegation. If you have team members, you should be giving them repetitive or non-value-add work that still must be done. Many managers hold on to too much work for a variety of reasons. Because of this, they become ineffective leaders. Be a delegator.

2. Hold other groups accountable

If you work at a company and someone else is responsible for a task, let them do it. Many go-getters gladly take everything on for a customer. Learning to let go and allow other employees to do their share can really free your time. This was a challenge for me, as I am perhaps a "control freak" in some areas. But once I started expecting more of coworkers, they stepped up, and my opportunities expanded widely.

3. Get help

If you are in a position to do this, get an intern, virtual assistant, or regular employee to take the "repetitive task" load off of you. There are cheap or even free ways to get the help you need, even if it's just for five hours per week. If you work for a company, you may still be able to take advantage of this option if it's within their rules. I did.

If you think cost is an issue, get over that. You have the math to show the value. But also consider that you can often bring on an intern for free. You will need to provide mentoring in return, but that's a bonus in my mind.

Alternatively, you can pay your assistants in a results-based manner. If they impact your results, everyone wins. Find someone who is looking to become a Grinder and have them help you out in areas where you're weak. For example, I'm weak at editing. I have a friend who is breaking into editing. It's a perfect match, and I can pay him a percentage of sales. It's simple and exciting for both of us.

4. Think professionals

Whether in your personal or business life, you probably have plenty of items you should hand off to a professional. For most people, spending time dealing with tax forms, invoices, and QuickBooks sucks. Yet many small-business owners I know spend hours each day on these non-value-add tasks. Instead of doing revenue-generating activities, they're back at the office dealing with paperwork. Additionally, since none of this is what they're good at, they're probably costing themselves money due to poor tracking, errors, and omissions. Hiring a bookkeeper and/or tax accountant can be life saving. These specialists will probably take one hour to do what takes you five. And they'll track it better.

When I coach people, I always encourage them to hire a bookkeeper. Invariably, they recognize doing so as one of the best decisions they've made. The bookkeeper pays for themselves many times over. Invoices are accurate and followed-up on. Expenses are tracked properly for taxes. And, the time saved is astonishing. If you don't yet have cause for a bookkeeper, find some other person (like a tax accountant) that you can hire, setting yourself free from a non-value-add task.

5. Don't stop at the office

Removing waste doesn't stop at the office. Cleaning the house, mowing the lawn, preparing meals, and numerous other tasks are all up for consideration. If there are household tasks you dislike, are causing trouble in your relationships, or are simply zapping your time and energy...have someone else do them! Chances are there is a kid in your neighborhood who would love an extra five bucks. Take that saved time and spend it with your family, on exercise, or on writing a book.

Exercise – Stop, Automate, and Delegate

"I don't have enough time to do that" should never be an excuse. If I ever find myself working too many hours, I simply pause and write down what I can push off to someone else. That is how you grow—you remove yourself as a limiting factor. Letting go also gives you more of your time back.

Are you choosing to do activities that prevent you from making the highest and best use of your time? Instead of saying "I don't have time," say "I need to stop, automate, and delegate."

Alright, you have everything you need. I want you to go through your data and pick one thing you can eliminate, one you can automate, and one you can delegate. Here are some final questions to answer as well:

Question 1

What is one non-value-add activity you will eliminate (stop doing)? How much time will this save you per day, week, month, and year? What's the dollar value you free up?

Question 2

What is one non-value-add activity you will automate? Remember, this can be automation via scripts, FAQs, documentation, and more. Get creative. How much time will this save you per day, week, month, and year? What's the dollar value you free up?

Question 3

What is one non-value-add activity you will delegate? This can be traditional delegation, having a coworker take their fair share of responsibilities, hiring a professional, or paying a neighborhood kid to take care of your lawn. How much time will this save you per day, week, month, and year? What's the dollar value you free up?

Conclusion and takeaway

These have been meaty exercises. Apart from helping you get over the major hurdles of time and money, they are also designed to show you how to efficiently run businesses. Baking these approaches into your standard behavior will cause you to avoid bloat and focus on what really matters from Day 1.

CHAPTER 7

Obsession

Goals

- Become obsessed with what you're going after
- Revise and update your goals
- Find ways to achieve your goals by attaching yourself to existing growth
- Evaluate your entire situation: your friends, where you live, and how you make money
- Understand food and dial in your eating
- Understand and commit to movement
- Uncover what will happen if you don't achieve your goals
- Set anti-goals that scare the heck out of you
- List out your wins so far from this book
- **Action:** Use the daily and monthly worksheets at *justingesso.com/52x*
- **Action:** Take at least one big daily action toward each of your Grinder-3 Goals

Obsession

Alright, you just finished an absolutely grueling chapter on optimizing your time and money. It wasn't easy, but it's something you simply have to deal with. But now that we have those excuses handled, it's time to have some fun. Get ready to light your fire.

> "Obsession is like a fire, you want to build it so big that people feel compelled to sit around it in admiration. Once the obsessed become successful, they're no longer labeled as crazy but instead as extraordinary. There's nothing wrong with being obsessed if you made a decision to be. BE OBSESSED FOR SUCCESS!"
> ~Grant Cardone~

In this chapter, we'll ramp up your obsession with life, your obsession with achieving your goals. This is the final stage before you nail down the business you want to create. Stirring up this final push of enthusiasm will ensure you take off with something you can really enjoy doing…something that you're able to put the needed energy into. It's time to make it happen like never before.

The concept in this lesson is stated many ways: focus, desire, burning desire, attention, or thought. But the one that hits home for me is obsession.

This is about being so excited and so consumed with your goals that you think about them all the time. They give you energy. They drive you crazy. Your brain is constantly chugging through them. You want to work on them day and night until they're complete. Opportunities seem to be everywhere.

When I first started talking to people about how I quit my job and launched myself, I spoke about "spinning myself up into a frenzy." I followed the principles here and got myself so wound up and so obsessed that I really had no other choice than to quit my job. I thought about it constantly. I talked to everyone about it. I was excited, enthused, and energized.

Obsession is a prerequisite for playing big

If you're chasing the wrong goals—perhaps goals you *think* you should have—you can't achieve the necessary level of obsession. The wrong goals will stress you out, drain your energy, and get pushed aside. You need to take a hard look at your goals then line them up to your mission statement. If you can't find excitement in them and can't sync them with a bigger purpose, you probably need to discard them.

But, if you even have a bit of passion and excitement for your goals today, here's how we're going to ramp that excitement through the roof.

Is this The Law of Attraction? Anyone who dives into the deep end of success literature has undoubtedly come across The Law of Attraction. In many ways, it is about obsessively honing your mind's focus on what you want. By doing so, according to this idea, you then get what you want.

If you become absolutely obsessed with what you want, things will happen. Whether something we don't understand is at play or it's just you kicking ass, I'll let you roll with whatever matches your personality.

But let me tell you…

...you will find opportunities you would have otherwise missed. You will connect with great people. And most importantly, you will take action. Big action. Fast action. You will get it done. Obsession puts you in the driver's seat.

This is why you hear about writing your goals down constantly, creating affirmations, and cutting out pictures of what you want. Whatever it takes to get you obsessed, do it.

If you want to do something big, you must be absolutely obsessed with achieving it. The size of your goal needs to match the size of your obsession, your focus, your desire, your attention, your thoughts, and your actions.

Your obsession is being used against you

Marketers understand obsession well. They use it to prey upon you. Because of it, you willfully hand over thousands and thousands of dollars. Kids are the best example. A new movie comes out, and it's awesome. It's all kids can talk about. They see the movie. They must have the toys, the costumes, the Legos, the themed birthday party, and more.

Apple, Disney, Tesla, and many others are masters of playing on obsession through marketing. Harness this power to achieve your goals, not the goals of some marketer.

 Exercise – Get Positively Obsessed

1. Review your life purpose and revise it.

Make your mission statement more personal. Ensure it speaks to you deeply. Why do you want to be great? Why do you want to do something big? Why are you reading this book? What really drives you?

2. Buy a basic notebook and write down *all of* your goals every single day.

Ramp the goal focus up. I do this while I drink my coffee in the morning. It takes a couple of minutes at most. You've already been writing down your Grinder-3 Goals. Now, I want you to write down as many goals as you can...every single day. Don't limit yourself to goals you want to achieve this month or year either. Let any life goals slip in.

Just write. Let it flow freely. See how your goals change and evolve each day. By doing this, you'll start to identify the goals that you're really excited about. You'll also be building an obsessive daily habit of thinking about your goals.

3. Ditch goals you can't get obsessed about.

As you go through this, you'll find that some goals you picked don't get you truly fired up. You don't want to think about those all the time. Ditch them and move on, especially if you've put them in your Grinder-3 Goals.

Attach Yourself to Growth

By this point in the book—especially because you've been making phone calls every week—you should have some opportunities you're either considering or already diving into. That's great!

So how do you wisely choose what you want to do? How do you make sure you get into a better situation than where you are now? Assuming your ideas and opportunities align with your mission and goals, that's a great start.

But what reduces your risk? Part II of this book is about establishing the right foundation. But it's also about placing your foundation in the right place. It is about attaching yourself to growth.

> "People are like dirt. They can either nourish you and help you grow as a person or they can stunt your growth and make you wilt and die."
> ~Plato~

Your external environment amazingly impacts your success chances. If you're surrounded by growth, then you're in a growing business, a growing city, and hanging out with friends who are growing. Your houses are appreciating. You can probably be a slacker and do good things in life. If you're a Grinder fueled by the information in this book, you'll explode.

On the other hand, if you're *not* surrounded by growth, your company is in cost-control mode, your city is old and stagnant, and your friends are happy to be Cogs. Well, even if you're awesome, you're going to struggle. You'll be fighting to swim upstream. Everything will be more challenging than it needs to be.

If you're joining a business, becoming a consultant for someone, starting a business, or investing in an area, you should look for one thing: growth.

Growth perspective as an employee

Let's consider a simple example. If you are considering two job offers, a massively important selection criteria for you is to determine which company is growing. Shrinking companies have problems. Steady-state companies have problems. And yes, growing companies have a lot of problems. But growing companies have good problems.

Working in a growing business environment can teach you massive amounts about how to scale a company up. It can teach you effective marketing and sales. And, since you will be growing with the company, you will be more indispensable and more likely to be called upon to take on more and more responsibility. You also are much more likely to be able to earn percentage pay and become rich.

Additionally, you'll find many other side benefits. Employees of growing companies are generally happier. Plus, money flows more freely, and empowerment is embedded in the culture.

How does working at a company that is not growing look? Downsizing and cost controls abound. All of the growth benefits I just described are flipped on their head.

People are in foul moods. Layoffs are common. Employees are competitive, bitter, and gossipy. Everything is a cost waiting to be cut. You may get more work and more responsibility, but that's because your coworker was just fired. You are likely *not* taking that on in exchange for more money or a promotion.

Growth perspective as a consultant

Let's now say that instead of being an employee for a company, you've decided to start a consulting business. You are seeking your first customer. It's important not to take just any consulting customer. Like an employee in a growing company, you need to target customers that are growing. You'll less likely be seen as a *cost* and more likely seen as an *asset*.

Further, as the company grows, their needs for your services will likely also grow. You don't have to go find new customers. Your consulting business grows merely because you have a growing customer base. Your life is much easier than if you're constantly justifying yourself, finding other new customers, and worrying about your future. By attaching yourself to a growing customer, your consulting business will simply expand with them. You have a base of success built into your business.

Growth and investing

Growth applies to many other facets of life, including investing. For example, if you're investing in real estate, you need to consider growth. Many "investor educators" say you cannot count on appreciation. They argue your entire focus should be on cash flow, which is the monthly income you receive from a property. While cash flow means great passive income and is a key metric I always evaluate when investing, cash flow alone simply won't make you rich.

Growth, or appreciation, should also be considered. An asset's growth in value is what will make you rich. Every single independently rich person I know became so through appreciation, not through cash flow.

Smart investors do, in fact, consider the long-term potential of their asset's location and its growth potential. Do people have reasons to continue to move in and drive demand? Can new house construction keep up? Are there good job sources? How diverse are the employers?

If you buy houses in growing areas that not only cash flow but also appreciate, you will become rich.

A great friend of mine is an expert real estate investor. He spent years picking fantastic properties that cash flowed phenomenally. In fact, he did such a good job that he was able to stop working and live completely off his investments' cash flow. Said another way, the cash flow he earned exceeded his expenses and allowed him to quit his job. Wow.

Yet many others who invested at the same time saw their net worth later explode. They became millionaires. While my friend's investments produced excellent cash flow, they were not in a growth area and had no real potential to massively increasing in value. While still successful, he did not become rich.

Upon seeing this play out, he internalized the need to consider growth. And he knew he couldn't do it in his part of the country. He needed to make a big move; otherwise, he'd stay on the sidelines. So he packed up his family, sold his investments, and moved halfway across the country to apply his knowledge in a *growing* geographical area.

You must be willing to make big moves like this to surround yourself with growth.

Exercise – Baseline Your Growth Potential

For this exercise, you'll baseline your current potential for growth. If you find some weaknesses here, you need to consider big changes, like switching jobs, moving to another city, or hanging out with different people.

Question 1

How do you rate your company's current growth? This applies whether you work at a traditional company, a startup, or for yourself. If you work for multiple companies, think about all of them, but concern yourself with the weakest link.

- My company downsizing and has been doing so for a while. Layoffs are common.
- Layoffs are in the air. New spending rarely happens. The company is constantly making changes but never really stepping forward.
- The company is fairly stagnant. It has a solid base and cash flow but isn't really leaping forward.
- My company is growing fairly well. We add new customers and revenue. Our problems involve handling all of the extra work and challenges that come with expanding our systems. Growth is in the range of 20% year over year.
- My company is exploding. We are not only getting many new customers, but we also have numerous new product and service offerings that the market is devouring. People are buying our products and services before they're ready. Marketing and sales are paying off big time. Our challenge is in meeting the demand and systematizing.

Question 2

How do you rate how your geographical location is changing? This has far-reaching impact on your ability to grow a business, invest, and meet the right people. Note that you don't need to live in a big city....just a growing one. For example, I live in a rapidly growing town, but houses here are still very affordable to me.

- My town is small and has been that way for the last 20 years. There are no big companies here. Things mostly stay the same.
- My city has numerous large companies that constantly hire. These companies may be stagnant or growing, but they're solid fixtures. Where I live, there is variety, diversity, and vibrancy. If I want to meet movers and shakers, there are plenty for me to choose from.
- I live in a boom town that is rated as a top-growing city by companies like Forbes or The Street. There are ongoing job and business prospects, making this an in-demand location.

Question 3

How do you rate your network in terms of growth?

- The people I hang out with and have access to are Cogs. They have jobs they don't like. They've been at those jobs for years. They don't make changes or take action. They complain.
- I have a mix of people in my network. Some are growth oriented, but many are taking a standard approach to life. I can join numerous clubs, groups, and societies to gain access to an even broader network.
- I hang out with growth-oriented people who are making much more money than I am. They maintain happy, fulfilling lives. I am part of clubs, groups, or societies that

allow me to interact with people who share a growth-oriented mindset. They are real movers and shakers.

Food and Movement

We've talked a lot about success, money, and time...but let's not forget the fuel that makes that all possible: your health and vitality. If you're having trouble becoming truly obsessed with life and generating the energy you need to build a business, you may not be giving your body everything it deserves.

I'm pretty sure you won't find this topic in an MBA program, but I can assure you that you you need to care for the vehicle that makes everything possible. Think about abnormally successful people across your network. Are they happy, vibrant, and in good health? The people I know who own growing, thriving businesses have serious energy and are deliberate about their health. Likewise, each of the coaching programs I have done—regardless of their primary purpose—addressed physical health.

If your energy wanes in the afternoon; if you don't have the focus to see goals through; if you have a hard time staying positive; or if you simply hit snooze too often, your health is not optimized. Your body is sabotaging you. So as unusual as it may seem to put a section on "food and movement" in a book on creating small businesses, I'd be doing you a disservice if I ignored these concepts.

The good news is, by deliberate choice and action, you can control and manipulate your energy, your health, your ability to focus, and much more. In other words, with a few simple changes, you can control your output. Knowing you are able to optimize your mind, your energy, and your drive is empowering.

In fact, I think we need struggles—and not just mental struggles. Our bodies thrive off physical struggle. Exercise provides a physical challenge that seems to unlock our overall potential. If you're stuck, mad, sad, or otherwise deflated, just go struggle through exercise...and win. Do something physically challenging. Your mindset changes. Your creativity opens up. Movement is key to my ability to keep pressing forward and maintain a positive, productive outlook on life.

Here is a great quote to get you started:

> "To lose one's health renders science null, art inglorious, strength unavailable, wealth useless, and eloquence powerless."
> ~Herophilus C. 300 BC~

And here's one from Anthony Robbins on health and energy:

> "The higher your energy level, the more efficient your body. The more efficient your body, the better you feel and the more you will use your talent to produce outstanding results."
> ~Anthony Robbins~

Before we move on, let me start by saying I'm not a health professional, and everyone has a different health situation, so make sure to run any changes by your doctor. In fact, if you really want to knock this section out of the park, go find a nutritionist who pulls blood work and runs other tests to dial in a precise plan designed just for you.

Chances are you have a food problem

According to an in-depth study on lifestyle and disease, fewer than 3% of Americans live a healthy lifestyle (*Mayo Clinic Proceedings*). Most other countries rate better...but not by much. What's interesting is 75% of Americans *believe* they eat healthily (*NPR*).

That's a massive gap in understanding. Some people simply don't understand food. You're probably one of them. And that's understandable. Nutrition is a messy subject that's constantly being tweaked and revised. Studies have agendas, and misinformation abounds. Fat is good; fat is bad. Carbs are good; carbs are bad. As a whole, we're all still learning a lot about the body.

But there are some simple principles you can begin to follow that will help you cut through the clutter. Food possibly makes the biggest impact on your overall life...in both the short and long run. Make sure you strive to constantly improve your understanding of it.

Find a purpose for maintaining good health

Go back to your mission statement. Look at your goals. You need to tie a long-term picture to your health. This is that emotional component of goals I mentioned. A goal to lose 10 pounds this year is a weak goal. If you have goals of being able to travel the world with your spouse when you're 70, run with your great grandchildren when you're 80, and write an epic novel when you're 90…now we're talking. Those are reasons to maintain good health.

Long-term vision mandates having good health. Your goals should make you think twice before putting junk in your mouth.

Food controls health, energy, drive, and weight

If you have a health problem, an energy problem, a motivation problem, or a weight problem, you need to change what you eat. Good food can prevent disease; bad food can cause disease. This is a liberating concept. Taking charge of your health is not complex. You simply have one variable to play with.

Many people falsely rely on exercise to give them health, energy, drive, and weight loss. However, exercise is something you do for maybe 5-10 hours out of your 168 hour week. That's only 3% of your time. Exercise is vitally important and has its place, but it's nowhere near as impactful as the food you put in your body that is being digested around the clock.

You're still a caveman

Evolutionary timeframes are long. Our digestive systems come from a day when we foraged berries, twigs, and plants. We also occasionally captured large animals and devoured them as part of a glorious feast.

What has happened within the last few decades, in terms of food processing, is not something our bodies have adapted to…not by a long shot.

With the caveman analogy in mind, the simplest nutritional advice I can give you is to only eat things that you can imagine coming directly from the ground and into your mouth. If you have to think too hard about where your food came from, don't eat it. That means most everything in the middle aisles of a typical grocery store is out.

For example, if I have some berries, I can imagine a farmer picking them and putting them in a box. Easy.

Now, if I have a candy bar, it's a different story. I can possibly imagine the peanuts coming from the ground. But, I can't even pronounce 80% of the ingredients, let alone know where they came from. If I was a caveman, could I have put this candy bar together? Heck no. In the trash it goes!

The lesson here is to eat simple foods. If you focus your diet on fruits, vegetables, legumes/beans, eggs, lean meats, and minimal oats/grains, you'll be rocking.

How the transition feels

If you're transitioning away from less-healthy foods, expect some trouble. For many people, a healthy diet dramatically increases fiber intake. You'll crave bad food. You might have trouble sleeping, be irritable, and possibly be hungry. But don't worry: these are all temporary problems.

Does broccoli make you gassy? That's temporary. Eat the broccoli.

Once you settle into a healthy diet, you'll quickly find *the opposite* becomes true. Candy bars will seem disgusting. You'll feel the soda on your teeth and polluting your insides. Donuts will put you in a productivity coma. Once you commit to a healthy diet and get over that initial hurdle, it becomes very easy to stick to. Unhealthy food will become undesirable.

Once this happens, life becomes easy. You get your energy. You naturally maintain a great weight. You feel vital, energized, productive, and happy.

Exercise – Commit to Good Fuel

Pull out your notebook and do the following:

Step 1

Write that you are committed to only putting high-quality food in your mouth from now on. Write down why this is important to you in the long term.

Step 2

I want you to get a book that excites and educates you about eating well. Ideally, this is a big hardcover book that shows you how and why to eat well and includes multiple pictures of great foods. If it's written by a doctor or nutritionist, even better. If it has a fad-diet name in the title, skip it.

Step 3

The last step was about getting a book to improve your understanding of nutrition. I now want you to find a great book dedicated to healthy, *fast* recipes. People regularly make poor food choices when they don't plan or are in a time crunch. The right recipe book will help you avoid this trap and stay on track.

Step 4

All this talk about food is getting me hungry. Are you ready to start now? Make this breakfast: eggs, spinach, garbanzo beans, and berries. The beans will help you feel full. Cook everything in a single pan. Throw on as much spinach as you like and warm it up a bit in the pan. Need some flavor? Consider garlic, turmeric, cumin, or even Tabasco (I can imagine where Tabasco ingredients come from). That's it. It's easy and and tastes awesome! Feeling better and ready to be productive?

The purpose of exercise

Now that we've covered properly fueling your body, let's talk about keeping it moving and strong for the rest of your life. Exercise is not about losing weight. Again, most active exercisers only do it about 3% of the time. Food is much more important when it comes to weight management.

But here's what exercise will do:

- Strengthen your body
- Allow you to keep moving as you age
- Improve your organs
- Help prevent disease
- Prevent injuries
- Boost your mood
- Skyrocket your energy

Also, as your body composition changes and becomes stronger, life will become easier. Your body will burn fat on its own throughout the day. You'll crave better food. Improvements in your health will snowball.

What does your daily motion really look like? Do you sit in front of a computer for eight or more hours per day? If so, you are spending a huge amount of time stretching the backside of your body while compressing the front. Your shoulders and hands are in strange positions and are over-performing repetitive tasks.

Or, do you work in a manual labor job? You're probably not doing much better than someone in a desk job. You're likely straining your back, knees, and shoulders.

This will all eventually sneak up on you and cause mobility problems. If left unchecked, you are on course to have a hard time getting out of bed when you're 50. Do you want to spend your golden years stuck in a chair, watching TV, and complaining of pain? Or, do you want to be active, traveling, and enjoying your grandchildren?

Thought of in this way, exercise is not just about lifting weights and running on the treadmill. It is critical preventative medicine that maintains your vitality and ability to move as you please. A huge yet under-emphasized value of exercise is its ability to keep you moving well into old age.

Making movement a habit

Starting an exercise program is easy, but many people have a hard time sticking to one. As we've discussed with other habits, you need to keep it novel, and you need to find a way to be deliberate about it until it becomes a habit you no longer need to micromanage; exercise should become part of your life.

Here are some factors to consider that may help you develop the habit of movement:

- Do you like to work out alone or in a group? My wife loves group classes. I prefer to work out alone.

- Do you like going to the gym or staying home? I love the efficiency of a home workout. My wife gets energy from being around other people and also thrives on the commitment going to the gym demands.

- Do you excel at a sport? Maybe taking karate lessons or playing in a league is vastly more exciting to you than hitting the gym.

- Do you have long-term goals and purpose for exercising?

I also want to reiterate the importance of variety. Personally, I need to constantly change my workouts to stay motivated. That means I need new information and ideas. Just like with nutrition and business, I read and listen to books that get me excited about trying new things.

And what about finding time? Is lack of time an excuse you use for not sticking to exercise? Drop that right now. Studies show that you are more productive on days you exercise. You can take time out to exercise yet still get more done. Find a way to stick to exercise—that's it.

Exercise can be highly efficient

Another major consideration is exercise efficiency. If you love the exercise you are doing, then skip this section. But if you are merely exercising for a result, then the exercise itself is no more than a tool. So why not use the optimal tool?

Are hour-long treadmill workouts the right tool? In fact, they are far from efficient. High intensity interval training (HIIT) has been shown to deliver in 10 minutes the same results as traditional cardio exercise delivers in 60. Killer.

And those weightlifting sessions that bodybuilders do? Guess what—they're probably not efficient for you unless you have the same goals, are supplementing with the same drugs, and have the same genetic propensities. Rather than following their model, you can perform big movements involving many joints to deliver much more benefit in much less time.

Kettlebell routines are a great example of efficient exercise. In a short time, I can get my heart pumping, strengthen muscles across my entire body, and address the mobility issues caused by my desk-jockey time.

In short, the prevalent exercise modalities you commonly see at the gym are outdated and massively inefficient. Don't assume more time equals more benefit. Learn the latest on exercise, and you'll be pleasantly surprised how efficient and simple great exercise can be.

Move all day

You know that "3% of the time" exercise notion? Here's how to hack that. Move constantly. Address mobility regularly. Bake movement into as much of your day as possible:

- Walk more
- Take the stairs
- Stand up more (I eat every meal while standing)
- Pace and wander while you take phone calls
- Stretch while you're at your desk

Remember how habits compound? These little movement tweaks compound too. A little walking every day will amount to thousands of steps by the end of this year. Your daily choices define who you will be, and movement is no different.

Exercise and obsession

Alright, exercise is here in the obsession portion of this book. How does this all tie together?

When you exercise, you go into a meditative state. It's just you and your body pushing through something challenging. Your mind is freed. You separate from your problems. You gain clarity. Your subconscious gets some free time to chug on your obsessions, your goals, your purpose.

Exercise resets your mind and renews your ability to be obsessed with what matters. Exercise allows you to live longer in the life you want, but it also enables you to live the life you want now. Some of my biggest epiphanies and best ideas hit me immediately after a great workout. For me, there's no better way to unplug, reset, and come back fully charged.

As an example, while writing this book, I've regularly hit a wall and gotten stuck. Did I give up? Or did I clear my mind and renew my obsession? As soon as I recognize a slowdown, I stop, hammer out 100 jumping jacks, and get back to it. I return reignited.

 ### Exercise – Commit to Movement

Step 1

Grab that notebook and write down the following commitment to exercise:

I am committed to making quality movement and exercise a part of my life because it will fuel my obsession and allow me to realize my mission statement to its fullest.

Step 2

Write down how you will incorporate exercise into your weekly schedule. Decide how you will make time for it, and put it on your calendar.

Anti-Goals

When it comes to becoming obsessed with your goals, almost all advice tells you to focus on what you want. Focus with laser-like precision. Focus on the positive like a mad person. But what if there is another massive motivational force out there?

> "The secret of success is learning how to use pain and pleasure instead of having pain and pleasure use you. If you do that, you're in control of your life. If you don't, life controls you."
> ~Anthony Robbins~

I term this concept "anti-goals." Anti-goals, quite simply, are the way to layer an additional type of motivation into your life. Whereas most authors and speakers talk exclusively about catering to our reward system, few talk about our powerful avoidance system. While focusing on the positive is nice, the reality is humans are very good at avoiding pain. So let's use that to our advantage.

After all, why do most people go to a job that sucks and deal with a boss they hate every single day? Is that their goal? No! They're *scared* of not being able to provide for their family.

And why do you wear your seatbelt every day? Do you have a goal of getting moderately hurt in a crash? No! You are *scared* of having some random event completely derail your entire life.

We all go to great lengths to avoid things we don't like or that will harm us. Fear is powerful—massively powerful. Anti-goals allow you to harness that power to make real, lasting change in your life.

Let me paint the picture by going back to my early career when I first got an inkling of exactly how powerful anti-goals are. As I looked around at my coworkers, I noticed several of them had been in the same job for years. I mean the exact...same...job. And they most likely had been sitting in the same chair too. Some of these people had been there for three five, or 15+ years.

They complained all day. They disliked change. They looked like corporate zombies. And...I was scared of them. More specifically, I was scared to death of becoming them.

I always had plans to work hard, earn promotions, and achieve great things. But nothing fueled me more than avoiding my coworkers' corporate-zombie fate. If I worked same job for more than a year, I started getting agitated and scared. Was I turning into one of them? Was I going to be there in three years! Heck no!

Anti-goals are more powerful than regular goals

Nearly all success ideas and recommendations focus on the "pleasure" side of the equation because it's sexier. Figure out what you want in life; then—go get it. Bam! That's exciting stuff!

Anthony Robbins is an exception to this. As the quote at the start of this section implies, he breaks down daily decision making at a subconscious level to either seek pleasure or avoid pain. I love the simplicity of this concept. And it's important to take charge of both sides of the equation; otherwise, you'll never be fully in control of your own decision making. You'll continue to make subpar choices and live a subpar life.

Imagine an overweight person sitting on the couch watching TV. Certainly they must know they'd benefit by standing up and doing a simple jumping jack, right? Just get some movement in while you watch. Simple. But it's easier not to, especially if you're only in charge of a portion of your decision-making process.

Now imagine that same person. What if a car comes crashing through the side of the house? Or imagine something even simpler, like a bee flying in through the window? Will that same person jump up and avoid whatever is about to happen? Absolutely.

Another powerful aspect of anti-goals is the emotional one, namely embarrassment. Most people can't stand being embarrassed. A great way to leverage this is to tell people your big, ambitious goals. On the day you quit your job, tell your coworkers you're leaving to launch successful businesses. The world shall know your name!

If you fail and end up back in your Cog job, you're going to be embarrassed. That is a lot to of pride to swallow. And believe me, you'll do a lot to avoid it.

What happens when something bad occurs? We experience a massive physiological response. Our bodies are designed to give survival instincts a huge amount of weight. We go to great lengths to avoid what scares us. Let's take that response and apply it to getting the life you want.

Anti-goals fuel habits

My good friend—the habit—is back. Every day, you're making small choices. These choices build upon each other and compound to big results...big results you'll realize 52 weeks from now. Thinking about it this way, habits either drive you toward a goal or toward an anti-goal. But here's the danger: if you don't identify the anti-goal, you may be inching toward it every day without realizing you're setting yourself up for trouble.

In other words, knowing both what you want and what you don't want makes decision making that much simpler.

Here are three real-life examples that cemented this concept in my mind:

1. Door One or Door Two

One of my martial arts schools was in the same strip mall as a bar. On a Wednesday evening, walking in from the parking lot, picking out who was going to the school and who was going to the bar was pretty easy. Healthy, happy, confident, beaming people walked in one door. Leathery, slouched, old, run-down people walked in the other. After work on a Wednesday, do you work out or grab a couple of drinks? This is a simple decision that has tremendous compounding potential. For me, this literally made me fear one of the two doors.

2. Gardening or Recliner

There are two types of retired folks in my life. One group sits in a recliner all day, watches daytime TV with the volume set to 98, and that's about it. The other group is happy, healthy, vibrant, and is actively engaged in their life. They may garden, paint, golf, travel, or whatever. They're maximizing their golden years. The further down the aging road you look, the more obvious the effects of compounding habits become. Sitting on a recliner scares me, so I make daily choices now to avoid ending up stuck in one.

3. Wasting Your Life at Work

Most of us spend the majority of our waking hours either at work, getting ready for work, or commuting to and from work. Remember those coworkers who sat in the same chair for years and complained constantly? Those people scare me. On the other hand, have you seen people doing what they love...as though it's not even work? That's amazing! Those people are energized and enthusiastic and don't seem to have much to complain about. If I'm not one of those people who is obnoxiously enthusiastic about what I do all day, what am I here for?

What scares me?

Knowing what scares me gives me huge motivation to make the right daily choices and also to do big things in life. Here's a quick-punch list of what scares me personally:

- Being a chair-bound retiree
- Being average
- Not leaving a legacy
- Being out of shape
- Not experiencing what life has to offer...I don't want to miss out on great relationships, travel, excitement, or adventure
- Being stuck in a stupid job I don't like

As I was deciding to quit my job, I was scared. But, unlike most people. I wasn't scared of failing. I wasn't scared of having to come crawling back if I screwed up. I was scared that by having a normal job, I was missing out. I was scared I was missing out on doing what I want to do in life. I was scared I was on a path to some money...but not huge money.

Staying in the standard corporate world became much scarier than leaving. Once I hit that realization, making the leap was easy.

Anti-goals also played a key role in the release of my first book, *Leave the Grind Behind*. Writing a book and having it fall into the abyss of hundreds of thousands of books on Amazon scared me! That's why I spent the time and effort learning how to make it stand out. This anti-goal helped me make it a #1 bestseller in numerous countries and categories.

Wait...what about positive thinking?!?

The Law of Attraction gurus out there are probably going to cringe at my notion of anti-goals. But by avoiding this topic completely, you're missing out on one of the two motivating forces available to you.

I don't want you to spend all day every day worrying about bad things, but I do want you to have a clear picture of what will happen if you don't take control of your actions and habits. Harness that massive power and put it to use.

Exercise – What Scares You?

Alright, you probably saw this coming. It's time for a list. Make a big list of at least 20 things that scare you. Think long term. Write them down as follows:

- Being an old, rotten couch potato who is stuck to a recliner with the TV blaring at 98 volume scares the crap out of me!

- Having to come crawling back to my corporate job after I make a massive exit announcement scares me!

- Releasing a book into the abyss of Amazon where it will never get noticed scares me!

- Forget about just trying to find a girlfriend...what if I spend the rest of my life alone?!? That scares me!

Get writing!

Bonus Exercise – See Your Anti-Goals in Action

Ready to inject some obsession in your anti-goals? This exercise will really cement their power. If you want to quit smoking, don't just say lung cancer scares you...go to a hospital and actually visit cancer victims. Talk to them. Decide right there if you want to turn out like them. Is that stupid cigarette worth that future?

If you're scared of being a corporate stooge, talk to coworkers who have stagnated in their jobs for years.

Get out and observe people who have made choices that snuck up on them. See what will happen if you don't take and stick to big, fast action.

Here's a favorite of mine when I'm coaching students who are second-guessing their decision to leave their corporate job. If you are thinking of crawling back to the regular W-2 world, go interview for a regular job. Look around the office and decide if that's what you really want. You will probably smirk and excuse yourself. This exercise will give you the fuel to come back and do whatever it takes to make your small business work.

Wins, Tally, and Recognition

Let's cement that obsession, passion, and fire within you! You've done a lot of work in Part II. It's time to wrap up, celebrate that effort, tally your wins, and recommit to yourself. Tracking wins is key to building obsession and maintaining momentum.

 ## Exercise – Wins Tally

When you're on a roll, it's easy to take big steps and not realize how massive they actually were. From time to time, it's important to stop, look behind you, and marvel at exactly how far you've come. Doing so leverages positive reinforcement and fuels your obsession that much more.

So let's do it now. I want you to write out your wins from Parts I and II of this book. If you want to get fancy, don't just write them in a notebook: pin them on your wall, write them on notecards, or create a winner's dashboard. Make yourself a plaque or certificate. Play this up.

Here are some "win" areas to consider. Have you:

- Created and stuck to new, positive habits?
- Obliterated bad habits?
- Written and tweaked an awesome life purpose that fuels you?
- Connected with new people or rekindled old relationships?
- Understood your values, how you're unique, and what drives you?
- Gained clarity in your life by establishing a master plan that covers the next one, three, five, and 10 years?
- Tackled unsupportive thoughts and mindset?
- Eliminated waste from your day, giving you time and money to create your future?
- Hired an assistant or professional?
- Become literally obsessed with achieving your goals?
- Taken a big action like changing jobs or attaching yourself to growth some other way?
- Cleaned up your diet?
- Improved your exercise and mobility habits?
- Become scared of failing to achieving greatness?

That's a pretty handsome list, but I assume you've accomplished much, much more than that. Get it all out in this exercise, which is easy and—hopefully—an absolute blast. Grab your notebook and write out at least 20 awesome "wins." Get crazy and obnoxious with your wording. Make this exciting. You should smile as you're writing these down. Stretch yourself to write 50 or

100 wins. Think of how much you've accomplished in life since you started this book, but don't limit yourself to what you've read here. What other great things have you done since you started? List it all out!

And then respond to this statement: I have picked a few key wins from my list and have done something special with them. Whether I went out to dinner to celebrate a specific win, created an award or certificate, or created a dashboard with a few select wins, I've done something to genuinely acknowledge the effort I've put in and results I've achieved. I'm the CEO of my own life. And just like a CEO at a great company, I've officially recognized wins.

- Yes
- Not yet

Part III

Selection

Part III Introduction

Through Parts I and II, you developed an understanding of the lifestyle you want to achieve and created a solid foundation for success. Now, it's time to choose the mechanisms that will fulfill your goals and mission statement. You'll take formative steps toward creating your money machine…your business, your product, your service. This is exciting stuff!

CHAPTER 8

Business Ideas

Goals

- Work through your strengths and determine what makes you marketable
- Identify the type of business you want to start now
- Identify the type of business you want to grow into
- Generate your list of business ideas
- **Action:** Use the daily and monthly worksheets at *justingesso.com/52x*
- **Action:** Take at least one big daily action toward each of your Grinder-3 Goals

Alright, now we get to the fun part! We are about to take everything you've done over the first half of this book and apply it toward finding your real value. We are going to find that idea that will enable the lifestyle you deserve.

> "To me, ideas are worth nothing unless executed. They are just a multiplier. Execution is worth millions."
> ~Steve Jobs~

But wait...have you been slacking on your networking phone calls? If so, it will start to show. The more I watch certain people succeed again and again, the more apparent the depth of their connections is to me. And of course, vice versa. As you'll see soon, humans will be fundamental as you start. Your big deals and opportunities will happen both because of your network and the trust people have in you.

The strength (not size) of your network is your make-or-break factor.

Have you been half-hearted about improving your relationships? Remember, the worksheets at justingesso.com/52x are there to help.

The 8 Characteristics of a Great Small Business

I hesitate to put up any limiting thoughts or boundaries at the start of this chapter because after all, Part III is about brainstorming. You should be wide open to ideas. So view these characteristics as inspiring, ideally causing you to identify unexpected opportunities.

In no particular order, here are eight characteristics of great small businesses:

1. Enjoyable

Based on everything you've seen thus far in this book, you had to see this coming. A small business needs to be *your* small business. It needs to be interesting, exciting, and enjoyable to you. It should fulfill your mission statement and give you the lifestyle you desire. During brainstorming, consult the lists and worksheets you've created throughout the course of this book for inspiration.

2. Niche Oriented

Businesses thrive when they target a very specific set of people and a specific problem. There's plenty of room to broaden later, but think specifically to start. Remember, Amazon.com started as an online book retailer., In fact, Jeff Bezos started by creating a list of 20 products he could sell online. He narrowed it down to one—books—and ran with it. The rest is history. As you brainstorm ideas, consider taking any one idea (such as selling online) and breaking it down into 20 specific ideas (selling books online, selling courses online, etc…).

3. Passive

If you earn income passively, your potential income isn't limited by your time. You put effort and money in up front, but eventually, you'll earn money indefinitely. This can be achieved through investing, owning intellectual property, automation, or hiring people. Even ideas such as consulting can grow and generate money without you as long as you're able to build the right team and systems to deliver. What ideas can generate money without your constant involvement?

4. Scalable

Much like passive income, scalable income is not limited by your time. However, it has another quality: the ability to hit massive quantities. If you can sell 100 or 100,000 products per month without much change in your direct effort, your idea is scalable. A rental property generates passive income but isn't scalable. A book that's exposed to millions of people is, however, scalable.

5. Sellable

Where's the big payoff? Selling! Not only can a business sell products and services, but the business can also be sold. Selling a business is a great way to realize a cash windfall. You can, for example, sell unique intellectual property, your customer list, or an income-producing asset. Investors buy businesses. Competitors buy businesses. Keep this goal in mind and think of ideas that will generate value for potential buyers.

6. Local Roots

In contrast to some of the bigger concepts in this list, many of the best ideas have their roots as local businesses. Being local allows you to spend time with customers and really understand what they need and want. With this deep understanding, you're better able to successfully go big and global with your ideas.

7. Tight Network

When your initial customers, vendors, employees, and partners come from your network, life is easy, familiar, and predictable. Great small businesses afford you the ability to add value to people who already trust you. You can start selling to people you are close to as opposed to cold, anonymous people. Likewise, if you can build your team and fulfillment process with people you enjoy and trust to deliver, the easier success will be. Similar to the "local roots" concept, building a business around your network allows you to start strong and create a rock-solid foundation before going big.

8. Paved Path

Contrary to what you may hear and expect, many of the best small businesses are not based on new concepts. Rather, great small businesses start on a paved path and introduce minor innovation. Creating a new market for a new idea or product requires educating huge numbers of people on your new concept, long periods of trial and error, and significant development work. In other words, it's insanely expensive and not where most of us will operate. So why not let someone else spend the money, create the market, and learn the pitfalls? Don't start from scratch. Rather, start with an existing business model that is already proven to make money, really understand why it's successful, and then implement it yourself with minor innovations. Follow a model. Find a paved path.

 ## *Exercise* – Capture Ideas

There is much more to come that will help you brainstorm and evaluate ideas, but did this first section get any of your creative juices flowing? If so, make sure to capture ideas in your notebook. Even high-level ideas should be written down. Ideas can be fleeting, and you never know how they'll evolve. Jot down at least 10 business ideas right now.

Marketable Skills

As we begin generating the right money-machine ideas for you, let's consider what it is you currently bring to the table. This is a fun, creative, and exciting exercise. And, it's massively important. We are going to use the information you create here from here out.

> "You don't set out to build a wall. You don't say 'I'm going to build the biggest, baddest, greatest wall that's ever been built.' You don't start there. You say, 'I'm going to lay this brick as perfectly as a brick can be laid.' You do that every single day. And soon you have a wall."
>
> ~Will Smith~

Before you get started, I do want to highlight that what you *don't* list here will be very important too. In an upcoming section, we will take the skills you identify here and uncover any gaps you're going to need to address.

 ## Exercise – Your Marketable Skillset

I want you to come up with a huge list, preferably of 30 or more items describing what you have to offer. I'll give you some questions below to get the juices flowing. At the end, you'll have something of a super resume. To get deep enough, it's important you engage your loved ones, friends, and professional network.

Grab your notebook, and let's go...

Question 1: What have people paid you for?

What people have paid you for in the past is a good indicator of what they'll pay you for in the future. Don't think about your job titles, but think about the activities for which you were responsible. People didn't just pay you to be a customer service agent—they paid you because you could resolve complex issues and build relationships with customers. What skills allowed you to accomplish that? Likewise, people didn't just pay you to pull reports out of some system—they paid you because you could extract and present meaningful data about a business to drive decision making. Why were you the right person to do this?

Next to each skill in this area, it's very important you jot down actual results in terms of a number. What business change did your contribution lead to? For example, perhaps you beat customer satisfaction targets by 50%. Or, perhaps because of your reports, your company reduced time-to-market delivery by 38%. At the end of the day, numbers matter to business owners, who are the people who will consider your services. For each skill you list, try to write down at least one numeric result you achieved. You need this information, so don't be hasty. Put in the time and do your homework.

Question 2: What big projects have you worked?

Any time you've been part of a larger project, you've likely seen a variety of disciplines come together to achieve a large goal. These projects provide a great learning opportunity and allow you to test your skills in a broader context. Which skills were you able to refine or develop during these projects?

Just like the first question, capture the numeric results of your actions and of the project as a whole. Businesses work because teams come together. If you were part of a team, capture the results the team delivered.

Question 3: What additional skills have you yet to flex?

What skills haven't you been able to use yet in a professional context? Perhaps you know a lot about a particular discipline or have developed a strong skillset in a particular area but haven't made any money from it yet.

Similarly, what do you enjoy doing? Perhaps something you do regularly in your free time has market value. Do you spend time reading about and practicing something just because you're extremely interested in it?

While this set likely won't have any numbers associated with it, think about what parts of a business you could impact. What business problems could you solve with these skills?

Question 4: What functional expertise do you have?

A final approach is to consider skills you have developed from an organizational perspective. Do you have expertise in marketing, finance, accounting, sales, operations, or product development? Consider the organization as a starting point. Be sure to get as specific as possible.

Refer to your list regularly

As you work through this chapter, continue coming back to your list and updating it. Your skills list is a great source of inspiration for business ideas.

Products or Services

I want to broaden your perspective on the available types of businesses there are for you to start. This should help remove any mental obstacles you have associated with perceived complexities. And no, this isn't about LLCs, S-Corps, or other boring terms.

> "Join the movement. The 9-5 job is over. Take control of your time, happiness and money."
> ~Success Magazine, August 2016~

This book is working you toward starting a business and profiting this year. That's a bold claim, especially when most people assume you need to invest large amounts of time and money to launch a successful, sustainable business. But the reality is your business doesn't need to be complex to generate money. And you can phase things in over time. Let's dive into what I mean by this.

Almost all businesses sell either a product, a service, or both. The one you choose will have a huge impact on your time-to-cash, amount of experimentation, start-up costs, and overall operational complexity.

Product companies

When it comes to products, don't just think something you can hold in your hand. Products span the spectrum, including software, shirts, supplies, systems, books...you name it. Selling products is awesome for many reasons. The two big ones are:

- You can sell in scale. If your product is well received, you can sell millions, which is exciting...even at low margins.
- You have intellectual property. This means you have an exit. You can sell the company thanks to the intellectual-property value. Big windfalls from the sale of a company can give you the fuel to take on your next venture at a much larger scale.

When people think about starting a business, they often assume they need to sell a tangible product. While I urge you to ultimately get there, it's the hardest place to start. Selling a product involves many downsides and complexities. Products often require major upfront time and monetary expenses, particularly in research and development.

You will have to think about logistics, manufacturing, and distribution. If you're selling a product, you almost always need to go big on marketing and sales. Competitors will emerge that already have these systems not only in place, but also heavily optimized. These companies can push you out of the market, drive down margins, and run you out of business. In fact, many companies sell products at a loss just so they can attach services later. The services arm becomes their cash cow, and products feed it. If you're not in a financial position to compete with this, you'll slowly die out. Are you ready to sell at a loss?

Additionally, if you take an idea to market, there's a good chance you will not have the depth of feedback to ensure the product is actually what people want. Many product flops come from people who have "great" products but didn't really understanding their target market.

I don't say all of this to discourage you from launching a product. Rather, I am strongly recommending you begin elsewhere if you're starting your first business..

Service businesses

Unlike product-based businesses, service businesses apply human skill and expertise to solve problems for other people or companies. The big downside most people see to service-based businesses is limited scalability. Most people assume they must be involved in the delivery of services and therefore will be limited by the time they spend delivering those services. Because of this, they see limits to the money their business can generate. But, this is a poor assumption. People also assume they will not generate intellectual property and will therefore be "stuck in the business" forever, with no real golden egg at the end. That's also false.

If you're just starting your first business and are looking to earn cash quickly, I cannot recommend starting a service-based business enough. Making money in this model is fairly easy and very lucrative. Doing so means you simply find the nexus of your skills and others' need for help.

Here is a rundown of the initial advantages to starting a service business:

- Startup costs will be minimal
- Time-to-start will be minimal
- You can sell both to your network and locally before you expand
- You can hire interns and assistants as you grow
- You can make real money now

- Your hustle makes the difference; you can play against bigger companies
- Customers have ongoing, recurring needs, creating long-term base income
- You will learn about a market in depth, allowing you to develop a great product and intellectual property later

That last bullet is important. One of the best parts of starting a service business is you get to be "in the weeds" with your customers. You learn their problems and their challenges. You can tweak and update your service on the fly. You can start to generate big concepts that later turn into larger businesses—perhaps even a product. Service businesses serve as incubators for golden eggs.

And I'd also like to elaborate on the ability to stand out and deal with competition. With a service business, you *can* compete with the big boys. Individuals and small businesses most always win on the services side. While undercutting on product with optimized global logistics might be easy, you can't copy an individual or local delivery. Through hard work, hustle, and an obsession with being the best, you can beat the large companies.

Service first, product second

As you build real-world service experience, you will gain more expertise, more customers, and more revenue. You will transition to working on the systems and processes that make companies successful. You will know your customers' and market's pulse. You will develop case studies, a strong network, and genuine expertise. You will have systematized many aspects of the work, allowing you to leverage interns or employees to help you grow. You will begin generating larger amounts of cash and commanding more for your services.

> "You can start selling immediately, with relatively little effort. I love service businesses because I'm impatient. I lose motivation if I can't see a quick path to profitability. These start-up companies that spend months or years developing their product and looking for funding scare me."
> ~Pia Silva, Badass Your Brand~

As your cash grows, so does your ability to generate a product based on your service. The solution you're delivering to your customers is your intellectual property and will become a product. You've already done the market research by spending time in the trenches. You know exactly what people want and what they're willing to pay for. You can afford risking going bigger on product development and logistics.

While most people think product first, service second, I have seen *time and time again* that the service-first approach rules the roost. So sell that awesome internet product after you've proven the concepts and battle-tested them by providing a service.

Let's say you have online-marketing expertise. You can consult for local businesses via introductions from people in your network. Your marketing efforts deliver real leads and deals. You become hugely valuable. While you might work as a Marketing Admin in the W-2 world, here you can run the show. You don't have to know everything—you just have to know enough to get started. You will learn immensely as you go. Over the long term, you'll dial in systems and processes and can productize what you've learned. Your product sells easily because it's based on depth of experience. It's truly battle tested.

Exercise – What Services Can You Offer?

Grab your notebook and list 10-20 local businesses and another 10-20 big businesses that have a decision maker in your network. What pain points do you see these business dealing with? What are they doing poorly? (By the way, this exercise is much easier if you're making your weekly networking calls.)

Next, go back to your list of marketable skills. How do these challenges intersect with your skills? Again, you don't need to be an expert in these areas. Maybe these companies just need someone who can lend a hand. Think big, small, and everywhere in between. Don't worry about the details (that's coming)...just get some ideas out. For each business, jot down as many of your skills as possible that might be of value.

Micro, small, and big business

Now that you have some ideas about services and products, let's talk business size. We live in an incredibly exciting time where the size of the business no longer really matters. Thanks to the Internet and simplified technology, we can all accomplish global reach like never before in human history. Again, this is what Success Magazine terms the "You Economy." It is the concept that you—as an individual—have the ability to sell your products and services to most places in the world. What used to require a big business can now be accomplished by you alone.

Though I want you to have massive aspirations and long-term goals, there is nothing wrong with starting small. Starting small allows you to be flexible. It reduces your startup costs. It helps you get paid faster. And, it doesn't mean you can't also become big quickly. The You Economy affords us the ability to start small, test, and grow with much lower risk—so why not take advantage?

Your small business can be a side hustle, self-employment, a one-man show, or you employing 50 people. Each of these constructs can be highly effective. The results are what matter—not the complexity.

One of the best business owners in my network started a service business, and he started small. Before creating the company, a CTO in his network (yes, your network is important) was having a hard time filling a software engineering role at his company. My friend knew he could find someone (network again), so he did. He provided software engineering staff augmentation as a service. He did this on the side while still working his standard W-2 job.

It was a great way to build recurring and relatively passive revenue. He started with one person, but this number quickly grew and allowed him to quit his regular job to focus purely on providing high-quality, hard-to-find people for niche software engineering roles. In a few short years, his company grew to a multi-million dollar business with operations across the globe. He now provides staff augmentation and managed services to some of the biggest companies around. Think big. Start small. Learn. Be big.

And...don't neglect your network!

Personally, I enjoy collecting micro businesses and watching them grow. I have income streams from more sources than I can count on my fingers and toes. I love starting up new projects and making them blossom. I'm constantly surprised by how easy—once you have the right principles in place—generating money on your own in this fashion is. Additionally, having multiple money machines means you have more income levers to pull and better risk-prevention diversity. While I also work on big business ideas, these micro businesses have afforded me the time and money to pursue bigger and bigger aspirations.

What's the point of this section? If you want to start a big business, go for it. But if you're worried about starting a business because you think that means you need to deal with complexity, an office, employees, the government, and all sorts of insurance...stop. You should feel relieved. Starting a business is easier and less risky than it has ever been before.

Business-Idea Brainstorming

Thanks to the work you've put in to this point, you're likely overflowing with ideas for where you want to go next in your life. But you also might be more confused than ever. So here we are—dedicating a section to identifying how you can begin making money from your passions, strengths, interests, and skills.

> "It is a common experience that a problem difficult at night is resolved in the morning after the committee of sleep has worked on it."
> ~John Steinbeck~

Let's start off with a simple concept: what does any successful business do? The answer is it both solves problems and adds value. So a great way to fuel your ideas is to constantly ask these questions:

- What problems can I help people with?
- What problems can I help businesses with?
- How can I improve people's' lives?
- How can I improve businesses' results (particularly sales)?

Here's an example. If you have online-marketing expertise because you know how to run ads on Google and Facebook, you can both solve a problem and add value. I guarantee you there is someone out there who has a fantastic product but doesn't know how to effectively advertise online. You can solve that person's problem of not being able to reach customers. You can also add value because for every $100 you charge, you help them earn $200.

I don't want you to begin getting into numbers, resulting in analysis paralysis. But do ask yourself: do you see *potential* to solve a problem with your idea? Do you see *potential* to add value?

Exercise – List 50 High-Level Business Ideas

For this exercise, I want you to brainstorm like crazy. Bring in your coworkers, friends, and family again. Think big and broad. Go back and look at your skills. What awesome business ideas come from your notebook lists? What silly little businesses do your friends concoct? Grab your notebook and write them all down. Come up with at least 50 ways you can solve problems and add value. Focus on the big and the small.

I also want you to sleep on it for a few nights. I devote an entire chapter in *Leave the Grind Behind* to "sleeping on it,", but I'll give you the short version now. Before you go to bed, stare at your list of skills. Stare at your mission statement. Stare at your goals, your affirmations, and other lists you've created throughout this book. Let the information sink in. Now, close your eyes and imagine your brain as a personal assistant. Imagine yourself handing over the lists you just absorbed. Ask your assistant to put a list of business ideas together and deliver them to you in the morning. Relax, go to sleep, and let your subconscious deliver some magic. Be prepared to have creative ideas pop into your head while you're in the shower, driving, or exercising!

In the next chapter, we'll run your ideas through the 52x Business Evaluator. But at this stage, don't think about the 5,000 reasons you think your ideas won't work. Just go big and relax.

Bonus Business Ideas

Alright, although I prefer to give you the tools to generate your own business ideas, I can't write a book with "small business ideas" in the title without actually handing you some. So here you go. This list is well worn by myself and people in my network. These are ideas for making extra money or completely replacing your income.

While there are many business-idea lists out there, most focus on *easy money*. As such, the ideas in those lists are usually subpar and only appealing to someone who likely won't succeed in generating money anyway.

The ideas here, on the other hand, are genuine. That means you could easily fail with any of them; but you could also use any of them to genuinely set yourself free. Every idea here requires you to hustle harder than the next guy, work smarter, take the time to educate yourself, and execute. You are going to rely on your network, and you must market and sell your idea!

Said another way, you're not going to find get-rich-quick, pyramid, or other guru/scam ideas here. These ideas will require your sweat and passion. But because most people won't put in the sweat and passion needed, you can win much easier than you think.

Remember, with the right idea, sweat, and passion, nothing is better than your own business at giving you the life you want, the money you deserve, and the creative outlet you need. You owe it to yourself to earnestly move forward today. You'll thank yourself this time next year. Perhaps, in 52 weeks, you'll be making an extra $50,000 on the side. Or, perhaps you'll be in a position to completely quit your day job and earn six-figure income multiple times over.

Alright, before I get into the ideas, let me set a little context for how these are framed.

How can a business idea make you rich?

Earning a little extra money on the side is one thing. Even if that extra money becomes a six-figure income, are you rich? Probably not. As you look at these business ideas, I'll provide info on how they can not only generate extra income but also make you rich. Here are the three concepts from the start of Part III that I'll focus on:

- **Passive**. This means your potential income isn't limited by your time. You put in effort or money up front but then begin earning money indefinitely. This can be achieved through investing, owning intellectual property, or by hiring people. Even ideas such as consulting can grow and generate money without you as long as you're able to build the right team to deliver.

- **Scalable**. Much like passive income, scalable income is not limited by your time. However, it has another quality: the ability to hit massive quantities. If you can sell 100 items per month or 100,000 per month, without much change in your direct effort, your idea is scalable.

- **Sellable**. Selling a business is a great way to earn a cash windfall. You can, for example, sell unique intellectual property, your customer list, or an income-producing asset.

You will find some of the business ideas are neither passive, scalable, nor sellable. This doesn't necessarily mean an idea is bad; it may be effective for you and your circumstances. But as you evolve and expand, strive to layer in ideas that have the best potential to set you free financially.

Group 1: Ways to make money online

> "Content is where I expect much of the real money will be made on the Internet, just as it was in broadcasting."
> ~Bill Gates~

The great thing about creating content is you can express yourself creatively, dive into a topic you enjoy, and easily do it on the side at your own pace. Done properly, the financial rewards can be very significant. Better yet, most online income-generating methods become more and more passive over time. While you might put in hard work to create the content and market it, you are setting yourself up for recurring revenue that won't require your daily attention.

1. Write a book and self publish

Don't knock this idea. I know many people who make $3,000 to $20,000 per month from their books. This number, of course, has no ceiling. Finding a topic you like writing about is probably much easier than you think, and it is very enjoyable. Apart from the revenue earned, you will have excellent content you can use in numerous other ways. You can establish yourself as an authority, and you'll also have the ultimate business card.

Books can be a great way to not only make monthly cash flow but also to gain surges in cash. Book launches, done properly, can sell thousands of copies. Let's look at the numbers for a good launch.

Books Sold During Launch Week	25,000
Profit per Book	$3.86
Launch Marketing Expense	($10,000)
Book Launch Week Profit	**$86,500**

Resources:

- With freelancers globally available on places like *Fiverr.com*, you have access to inexpensive yet professional editing, cover design, and formatting at your fingertips.

- Once you have a great book, the real trick is marketing. Authors are called "best sellers" not "best writers" for a reason. I recommend *Epic Launch*, which I used to learn about selling books.

- In my experience, recording your book in audio format doubles your monthly income. You can have this professionally done on *ACX.com*, or you can use free software such as *Audacity* to do it yourself.

- Once you have a book idea, tools such as *KDP Rocket* help you analyze how many people are searching for your concept and keywords. While this is a paid tool, it will help your market research tremendously.

Can it make you rich?

- Passive: Yes
- Scalable: Yes
- Sellable: In most cases, no

Action: Brainstorm 20 ideas you'd enjoy writing about. Search for similar books on Amazon by category. Within the top 20 books in each category, what does the competition look like? If the top books don't have many reviews, you have a great chance of breaking in and standing out. Are there books with fewer than 20 reviews? Fewer than 10? If you find a niche to exploit, take the bonus actions of investigating search volume and creating an outline for your book.

2. Create a niche website

The goal of a niche website is to write about a specific topic in order to become a valuable informational resource. Niche websites earn money from affiliates and display advertisements run by Google Adwords or Facebook. Startup costs are as low as $5 per month for the hosting. You may know a lot about the topic, or you may just enjoy it. Regardless, you'll shoot to answer common questions people have through a combination of both your experience and research. Perhaps you want to write about bowling techniques, raising chickens, or fermenting your own probiotic foods.

Traffic generation is key to success. The content can be delivered in the format you find easiest to work with, be it video, written word, podcast, or otherwise. In fact, this content can come from a book you've written. Or, your website content can later become a book. Content can be packaged in numerous ways, which is why it is so important to just start creating.

Resources:

- Web hosting: *GoDaddy* offers great, inexpensive web hosting and excellent customer service.
- Email: *Getresponse* forms the backbone of your online business (your email list).
- There is plenty to learn and many subtleties to consider. *RankXL* is the best educational resource I've seen.

Can it make you rich?

- Passive: Yes
- Scalable: Yes
- Sellable: Yes

Action: List at least 20 topics you enjoy and could see yourself writing about. Then, study up on "keyword research" and see if any of your ideas are consistently searched for but not already dominated by big national companies. If you're having trouble, you probably just need to go a level more specific with your ideas. There are countless ideas out there that aren't yet saturated.

3. Sell an online course

If you've written a book or created a niche website, a natural progression is to create a course from that content. Online courses have higher value because they can be interactive, include multimedia, and even offer access to the creator (you). Online courses can be sold on your own website using a Learning Management System (LMS) or through marketplaces like Udemy.com. Depending on the delivery type, you can even charge monthly membership fees for recurring revenue.

Resources:

- Web hosting: *GoDaddy*
- Email: *Getresponse*
- LMS for Wordpress: *LearnDash*
- Payment Platform: *Stripe*

Can it make you rich?

- Passive: Yes
- Scalable: Yes
- Sellable: Yes

Action: Outline a four-module course in your area of expertise.

Group 2: Home-based business ideas

Most of us have the ability to run highly effective businesses from the comfort of our own home, whether on the side or full time. Though most ideas in this list can be done from home, here are some common approaches.

4. Consulting

Consulting is probably one of the best ways to create a small business or side hustle. If you've built experience in a particular area with results to back it, you can almost certainly begin selling your services. In fact, many companies that seek consulting services have little to no expertise in the area they hire out. They often just want the basics and don't require years of highly focused experience.

Generally, consultants earn twice as much as regular employees. That means if you're a marketing employee earning $50 per hour, you'd likely fetch $100 per hour as a consultant. Companies do this because they don't have to worry about the overhead of having employees (benefits, time off, management, building space, and more), and they also can disengage at any time. You, on the other hand, earn higher pay and enjoy more autonomy and greater control. It's fantastic.

Consulting is probably the simplest way for most people to transition out of regular employment. And if you build a business around it, it can grow independent of your time. That's right—you can charge $100 per hour and pay assistants $15 per hour to fulfill most of the services. This is how you can go from spending 40 hours per week selling to spending 400 hours per week. Your assistants help you scale the time investment. Not bad.

Can it make you rich?

- Passive: Yes, once it becomes a business
- Scalable: No, but your expertise can be spun off to books, software, and more
- Sellable: Yes, once it becomes a business

Action: List 20 people in your network who are responsible for making purchasing decisions at their company. Brainstorm the value you can provide each of them. Reach out by phone to let them know you're considering starting a consulting business and would like their input on your ideas. Let it roll from there.

5. Coaching

Similar to consulting, coaching is a great way for many people to make money from home and on the side. Whereas consulting targets businesses, coaching targets individuals. But, you may find it more challenging to get off the ground than consulting.

Specifically, the challenge is budgeting. Businesses tend to have budgets and clear consulting plans, but many individuals do not set aside money for coaching. Therefore, coaching is typically a bit tougher sale. You must demonstrate deep expertise in an area and be able to reach people that value personal investment.

Additionally, if people are paying for time specifically with you, there is less you can outsource.

Despite these challenges, coaching is highly rewarding. Taking part in personal transformations is fantastic. You will also learn a great deal about people's challenges with life and success. As a result, you'll likely uncover new avenues for your own success and businesses.

If coaching is something you're interested in, consider a certification program to increase your marketability. You can become certified by coaching programs such as the ones offered by Jack Canfield, T. Harv Eker, or Tony Robbins.

Resources:

- *Jack Canfield Train the Trainer*

Can it make you rich?

- Passive: No, unless you sell corresponding courses and books
- Scalable: No, unless you use at as a launching point to create a brand and follow-on products and services
- Sellable: No

Action: List your 10 personal areas of excellence and go through your numbers-based track record in each. Read up on coaching certification programs.

6. Freelancing

If consulting and coaching seem too tough to break into given your current experience, success record, time, or money, then freelancing is your answer. In fact, you can build a full-fledged business around freelancing.

Whether technical, artistic, or otherwise, there are millions of people seeking basic services on a one-off basis, services you can fulfill. These services are best kept very specific, such as designing logos, converting videos, formatting books for Kindle, or transcribing audio for podcasts.

Unlike many of the other ideas here, there are large marketplaces built around freelancing, such as Upwork and Fiverr.

This means people can bring their wallets, search, and find the services you provide. Marketplaces eliminate a big piece of the sales puzzle for you, but you will need to spend time learning how to compete. You need to figure out how to show in the top of the results for your speciality. Additionally, since you'll be competing globally, you will likely have price pressure.

Ultimately, you should leverage freelancing to build your experience, polish your business acumen, and develop relationships. By over delivering, you may find yourself moving into longer-term business relationships with clients. Freelancing should be used as a way to move up the chain.

Resources:

- *Fiverr*
- *Upwork*

Can it make you rich?

- Passive: No
- Scalable: No
- Sellable: No

Action: Go to fiverr.com and search gigs. Research areas in which you have expertise and interest. How competitive are they? What sort of prices are charged (you have to click past the basic gig prices to read true pricing)?

Group 3: Businesses from your trade or profession

Whether you are a plumber, software engineer, or CPA, chances are you can go out on your own. Rather than build your employer's future, build your own.

7. Skills-based service businesses

Over the years, as you've gained experience in your trade, you've likely built a network of people who know and trust your work. This is a great sign that it is time to go off on your own.

I know numerous business owners who created skills-based service companies. From HVAC to software companies, they've agreed it was the best decision they ever made. Creating a service business will not only build wealth but will also allow you to reduce your own time in the trade, which can be very important in manual-labor jobs as you age.

The other great thing about skills-based service businesses is specializing and avoiding competition is easy. You may only offer your services to a particularly underserved industry. Or, you may go local or hyper local. There are countless ways to slice-and-dice your target market, which will significantly help your chance for quick profit. Additionally, older companies providing these services become complacent all the time. Outshining them can be easy.

The idea here is to make money off of your employees while also retaining a higher rate yourself. Let's use plumbing as an example. As an employee, you might make $25 per hour. But, you'll notice that your company bills out work at $60 per hour. Let's see how that plays out:

Bill Rate	$60
Employee Pay	($25)
Overhead (20%)	($12)
Net Profit	**$23**

You'll see that the company keeps about the same profit as you. This model shows a 38% profit margin, which is very achievable for well-run companies.

Now, if you were to own a service business rather than work for one, here's how those numbers might play out. Let's say you have five employees delivering billable services. You will have an answering service, insurance, marketing, vehicle, and other costs, but those are wrapped into the overhead figure. We'll use the same assumptions as above.

	Assumption	Monthly Dollars
Employee Time Billed	800 hours per month	$48,000
Your Time Billed	100 hours per month	$6,000
Employee Pay	$25 per hour	($20,000)
Additional Overhead	20% of billed	($10,800)
Net Profit	**Monthly**	**$23,200**

These numbers show that you've reduced your billable time to about 25 hours per week. Perhaps you work another 10 hours per week on the business. Meanwhile, your annual pay has gone from $50,000 to $278,400.

This may all start with one employee, building up to five over time. Ultimately, your billable time decreases, and perhaps you even hire a manager, thereby allowing you to enjoy time away from the business. It's easy to see why this is such a great model. It allows you to ease in and offers a clear exit.

Can it make you rich?

- Passive: Yes, once you step out of the day-to-day processes

- Scalable: No
- Sellable: Yes

Action: Get over your fear of creating a business. If you're an HVAC technician, the idea of creating a website to get business may be prohibitively daunting. Don't let it be. Search local marketing companies, set appointments, and let them know what you're up to. See what they can do for you. You might be pleasantly surprised at how easy it will be to keep yourself and your first employee busy.

8. Create a software product

If you are a software engineer, creating software that makes a company money, you need to seriously consider creating software you can sell yourself. Some of the best and most exciting entrepreneurial ideas right now are coming from the software industry. Further, some of the largest acquisitions take place in software. Software engineering is a tough, competitive field, but people are making big money on the side or full-time all over the place, so why not you?

If you're able to provide software that addresses a problem or adds value to people, that is a great first step. The next step is marketing and selling the software, which is not easy. While there are many marketplaces (such as app stores) that allow you to distribute software, they are crowded, and there is price pressure. Take the same approach as you would when publishing a book: hire a freelance artist, copywriter, and others to fill in your gaps and develop a professional-quality product end to end. Then, you'll need to study up on how to compete in the various marketplaces or consider partnering with someone who has expertise in selling software.

Can it make you rich?

- Passive: Yes
- Scalable: Yes
- Sellable: Yes

Action: Research software-product monetization methods. Do you try to sell your product to businesses for immediate revenue? Or do you offer your product for free in an attempt to build a massive list of registered users? Or do you do something else? Start with a goal in mind in order to treat this as a business.

Group 4: Business ideas in real estate

Real estate is a fantastic place for prospective business owners to start. There are many ways you can use your a real estate license to make money. You can be exposed to very high, passive income and learn what it takes to run a business. Some of these ideas do not require you to have a real estate license, but all benefit from it.

9. Buy rental properties

Owning rental properties is a fantastic business model, allowing you to build passive income and wealth. As I like to say, not every real estate investor I know is rich, but every rich person I know is a real estate investor. The trick is to properly educate yourself.

When you buy a rental property, you are providing a service: you are providing housing to someone who cannot buy housing themselves. That is a great thing and very satisfying in and of itself. But it is also lucrative.

In order to not only earn passive income through monthly cash flow but to also get rich, you need to do one of two things: increase the income from the property or buy in a growing area. Those two things make the property more valuable and will allow you to sell for much more than you bought.

To succeed here, you don't necessarily need a lot of money—you just need that education.

Resources:

- Ben Leybovich. Get started at *justaskbenwhy.com*. Ben started with almost none of his own money and has built a great property portfolio. Oh and he no longer needs to work a regular job. He drives a Tesla, and he lives in a beautiful house...all thanks to real estate.

Can it make you rich?

- Passive: Yes
- Scalable: Probably not...unless you're buying large complexes
- Sellable: Yes

Action: Talk with a real estate agent (free) to learn typical rental-property profiles in your area, including the price point. Then, talk your bank to see what it would take to get a loan in place. If their requirements (cash or otherwise) are too high for you, research creative financing—there is always a way to get started.

10. House hacking

I love this one. A newly emerging trend is to use your house as a way to generate cash. This may offset some of your monthly mortgage payment, pay for your house completely, or provide very solid income. The trick is to find a primary residence that is suited for house hacking.

Do you think moving downtown or to your dream city is financially out of reach? Maybe not! Consider buying a house suited for house hacking. You can upgrade your lifestyle without breaking the bank.

Or, if you're younger, it may mean buying a house and having your college buddies live with you. You'll pay for your house using rent. Once you move on, you can sell the property or retain it as a rental.

Regardless of the approach you take, house hacking can allow you to earn income and build wealth through your primary property.

Resources:

- Advertise on *Airbnb* and *VRBO*
- Read the book *House Hacking*

Can it make you rich?

- Passive: Yes, assuming you build in a fee for cleaning and turnover service
- Scalable: No
- Sellable: Yes, as demonstrated income typically increases the value of your house

Action: Browse Airbnb and VRBO to see what type of properties are available in your ideal city. Call a local real estate agent to discuss the idea.

11. Fix and flip houses

Fixing and flipping is a great way to earn surges of cash. If you live in an appreciating market, where buying rental properties is hard, then this may still be a great way for you to make money in real estate. Despite what you see on TV, this is labor and money intensive. And there is no shortage of ways for things to go wrong. Finding deals can be challenging, especially if your market is saturated with other flippers. You'll also need a great network of reliable contractors, real estate agents, wholesalers, and more.

Resources:

- Mark Ferguson of *investfourmore.com* is the best and most active house flipper I know. He generally has 16-20 flips going at any one time, which is crazy! Maybe that's why he has a garage full of exotic cars. Get on his email list. You won't regret it.

Can it make you rich?

- Passive: No, unless you have a team doing the work for you
- Scalable: No
- Sellable: No

Action: Start educating yourself on the nuts and bolts of flipping. Learn the common numbers and ratios successful flippers utilize for property analysis.

12. Build a real estate team

Are you a real estate agent or are considering becoming one? That's great! Like other commission-based fields, real estate agents can make a whole lot of money. The key to making the income more passive is to build a team. That means you have other agents that work for you and give you a percentage of their commissions. Just like the plumber example above, this allows you to multiply your income and reduce your time.

What do you need to provide in exchange for the commission split? It's not as much as you think. Most new agents struggle with systems, structure, and lead generation. It's the basics that they must muddle through. You can provide answers, templates, a CRM, and other systems to fast track their success.

Resources:

- Mark Ferguson with *investfourmore.com* not only has great info on flips but also a ton about agents and building out teams.

Can it make you rich?

- Passive: Yes
- Scalable: No
- Sellable: Yes

Action: Talk to your Managing Broker about how building a team works in your office. Find some young agents who need some guidance, and see if they're interested in learning from you and being part of your structure.

13. Property management

Surprisingly, one of the wealthiest real estate agents I know is a property manager. Done right, property management can be an excellent business. Why? Because of the network you establish!

Think of the clients you will have. They will be people rich enough to have a portfolio of real estate they don't want to deal with. As a property manager, you have the opportunity to surround yourself with successful, business-minded people. Think of the opportunities that may come of that if you develop relationships properly and over-service them.

Additionally, the main income shouldn't come from property management fees. Your clients will be buying and selling houses regularly. The bulk of your income will actually be in commissions, not management fees. This is how you land multi-million dollar property contracts and have repeat customers in real estate.

Can it make you rich?

- Passive: Yes
- Scalable: Yes
- Sellable: Yes

Action: Take a property management class and attend a property management association meeting.

 ## *Exercise* – Expand Your Idea List

From the last section, you should have a list of 50+ ideas. After going through some of my ideas here, you should make additions and tweak your list. Whether you grab an idea from my list directly or your creative juices were stirred, add another 5-10 ideas to your list. Likewise, go back and refine a few of your best ideas.

Get Specific with Your Ideas

By this point, you should have brainstormed your own list of business ideas and reviewed mine. Now, let's begin getting as *specific* as possible with them. This specificity applies to what you offer and to whom. We want your idea to have a clear message and a clear audience. You'll commonly hear this referred to as *finding your niche*.

"Getting specific" creates a lot of advantages for you as the business owner. It is one of the best ways to overcome competition. The more general you are, the less you'll stand out. The more specific you are, the faster you'll realize success.

And don't think of specificity as limiting. You can always grow and expand. There's always room to think big.

Here are some ways to get specific with your ideas:

Start locally instead of globally

As you'll see in the upcoming Business Evaluation chapter, there are many advantages to starting a business locally. You can better learn about your customers and can rely on your network. Going local also helps your competitive chances. Start in your backyard and watch yourself grow into the big dog in no time.

Google Keyword Planner is an exceptional tool for finding local opportunities and gaps. You'll need to create a free Google Adwords account, but once you do, you'll be able to see precisely what customers are searching for and how competitive the advertising landscape actually is. It also allows you to drill into specific geographies, such as cities and counties.

I have used this tool to uncover numerous diamonds in the rough. Not only do I see how people actually search, but I may also find that a specific need is saturated in my city yet wide open in the next city over.

Get specific about your customers

If your business idea is not local by nature (book, course, software product), you need to get hyper-specific regarding the target audience and the problem you'll solve for them. Solve a problem for a specific person in a specific place. Advertise to them. Sell to them. Really get to know them. Eat where they eat and do what they do.

Dive into the demographics. Are you selling to retirees or college students? Are the college students at universities or community colleges? What are their majors? What are their hobbies and interests? Who do they follow? Try to ask at least 10 deep questions.

If you need some ideas on diving into your target audience, look no further than Facebook. It is the king of demographic and interest-data tracking. You can simply click "Boost" on one of your posts, and you'll see the option to target who will see your promoted post. As you begin typing in interests, Facebook will start making suggestions which can help you gain further insights into who your audience is.

Drill into what your audience specifically wants

Within your niche or business idea, what precisely do your customers want? Where are their interests, and how can you refine your concept to precisely meet these needs? What are your customers already willingly handing over their hard-earned money in exchange for?

Recently, I read through an "Ask Me Anything" forum session featuring a multi-millionaire app developer. When asked how he gets his ideas, he responded, "I look at the top app charts almost every day to have a look at what people are downloading these days. That gives me a good idea of what people would want."

This answer was beautiful. He was not assuming what people wanted; he was deep in it daily, looking at real data. Does this mean you just need to chase customers and money rather than follow your passions? No. But one day, you'll find that moment of inspiration—that moment when your enthusiasm and passion cross with what people specifically want. Something clicks and you make that one tweak that puts your ideas in sync with your customers. That's gold.

To understand your audience's actual behavior, you need to go where they go and gather data. Whether through the app store, Amazon, somewhere in person, or Google keyword research, go where your audience goes, and do the research.

 ## *Exercise* – Revise Your Business Ideas

Go back through your list of ideas and drill down into some of your favorites, making them more focused. How can you apply specific locations, specific customers, and specific wants?

If one of your ideas is to *start a marketing firm*, you may want to expand that to *start a marketing firm that generates leads for house-repair professionals in Ashland.*

CHAPTER 9

Business Evaluation

Goals

- Decide on 10 product or service ideas
- Apply real-life analysis to your business ideas using the Mission52x Business Evaluator
- Gain a deeper understanding of who will pay you
- Understand your competition
- Identify the strengths, opportunities, and pricing in your market
- Identify how your business will make money
- Determine the key variable to press on to achieve profit and your goals
- **Action:** Use the daily and monthly worksheets at *justingesso.com/52x*
- **Action:** Take at least one big daily action toward each of your Grinder-3 Goals

Alright, it's time to roll up your sleeves. We're about to get into the nitty gritty and apply real-world business-success principles to your ideas. This is your introduction to the *Mission52x Business Evaluator.*

"An Ivy League Education costs about $252,000 and will teach you exactly how to make a $60,000 per year salary." ~Bloomberg, 2015~

But before we start...

Business-idea analysis is a joke

This one pains me. I have an MBA. I spent a *lot* of time and effort dissecting businesses and learning theories on what it takes to have a successful company. Professionally, I've been at the table for countless business and product launches, with analysts and executives spending months pouring over data, diving into complex calculations, going through cumbersome governance meetings, and perfecting multi-year financial projections.

Smart people, countless hours of research and planning, and flawless market research invariably culminate in an idea that hits the market, immediately takes a left turn, and goes somewhere entirely unexpected.

While I'm not saying this type of analysis is worthless—we all need to understand our numbers, our levers, and how we'll make money—I will say the factors that cause a business to succeed or fail are much more basic and fundamental than most people think.

"In preparing for battle I have always found that plans are useless, but planning is indispensable." ~Dwight D. Eisenhower~

I am now in an environment steeped in people launching small-business ideas. The factors I see that determine success have much more to do with the owner, their environment, and the idea's ability to generate cash quickly. After all...the only reason businesses fail is because they don't make money *fast enough*.

This is good news for you. Your drive, hustle, and ability to get obsessed will make more of a difference than anything else. You have the tools within to beat the competition. If you do more, press harder, and drive faster, you will rise to the top. People and companies become complacent all the time. There's always opportunity for you to win.

With all of this in mind, I have put together an idea-evaluation framework that brings in the best from classical business analysis, but more importantly, also focuses on bigger-picture aspects. It will chug through your ideas in four phases. Once you've gone through the evaluation, you will have much better insight into your ideas and a real concept of whether or not they will succeed in your environment. So let's get started and look at the factors that really matter.

Evaluator Phase 1: Offers

 ## *Exercise* – Offer Evaluator (Phase 1)

The purpose of Phase 1 is to explore potential businesses to *offer* to your market. This scorecard will allow you to think through success factors and rank your ideas accordingly. This tool will give you a great sense of which business ideas you can best bring to market. It makes up Phase 1 of 4 in terms of your business analysis.

I recommend grabbing the top 10 ideas from your business-idea list and running them through Phase 1. You can certainly do more or less, but for your initial pass, 10 is a good starting point.

Alright, let's get to it. Download the *Mission52x Business Evaluator* at justingesso.com/52x. In the Phase 1 tab, list your top 10 ideas down the rows. You will then simply score each idea by the variables (columns) listed in the sheet. For each column, you'll assign a score from 1-10. I provide guideposts for scoring a 1, a 5, or a 10. These scores will be automatically multiplied across each row, providing you a comparative score at the end for each idea.

Here are the column details:

Offer description

List the 10 potential business ideas (services or products) you're considering selling. Describing each in a sentence forces you to clarify what you're really offering.

Skills

How well do your existing skills align with this offering?

- 1: I know almost nothing about this. I would need to build my knowledge about the core concept and then outsource all of the setup and delivery.
- 5: I understand this area and have strong skills in the core offering. I am not sure how to deliver it though (such as creating a website, marketing, fulfilling); I would need to outsource the delivery.
- 10: I have a very strong skillset in this area and also know how to deliver it end-to-end.

Interest

Rank your personal interest and excitement about this offering. Does it align with your mission?

- 1: Maybe I know how to do this and have strong skills here, but this just doesn't excite me at all.
- 5: I like doing work in this area well enough. If someone paid me good money, I'd gladly do it.
- 10: I obsess about this and would even do this if I wasn't assured payment.

Metrics

Rank your proven track record in this area.

- 1: I've never really done this in practice. I do not have testimonials or metrics to back up why I'm an expert.
- 5: Based on previous jobs and projects, I could probably scrape together a few testimonials and hard metrics (business numbers that changed as a result of my involvement) that would demonstrate my expertise.
- 10: I have led significant transformations in this area. I have hard-dollar figures demonstrating the value I deliver and clearly making me an expert.

Business

Can this offer be turned into a scalable or passive business?

- 1: This is a pretty specialized area that only I can really work. The end-to-end delivery would take all my time.
- 5: I can identify areas of this offering that could be picked up by automation and assistants. I could see running and

growing this business but spending little time on the delivery side.

- 10: This is something that could be fully automated. I would only need to work on sales and marketing, but ultimately, this has enough strength that those functions could be hired out. This can be scaled.

Local

Are you able to offer this product or service to local people and businesses? When you start a business, it is much easier to sell locally, in person, and to people who are part of your network or extended network. Additionally, this will give you the ability to see the customer in action and tweak your offering before going big and national. It's easier to stand out and start locally.

- 1: I don't really see this as something I could sell to my local network or local business owners.
- 5: It would take networking effort on my part, but I should be able to get a few local clients.
- 10: I know local people in my network who would benefit from this offering.

Competition

Rank your existing competition. We cannot be scared by competition; it's always there. But we should understand it. And remember, if you have a clear mission and are obsessed with it, you'll push further than 90% of the people. Others become complacent and are uprooted by new offerings all the time.

- 1: By doing a Google search for my offering, I see the front page covered with three paid placements (ads) or more. Pages one and two of the search results are littered with a mix of local and national companies in my space. Companies are competing on price.

- 5: There are 1-3 other local companies. Online searches yield some ads. Companies in search results are national, not local. Companies are competing on value and services, not price.

- 10: I'm not aware of anyone else delivering this offering. After doing some research, I'm sure most professionals and businesses don't have a reliable, qualified, local resource to use.

Validation

Do people want what you're offering?

- 1: I've asked around, but no one has provided a strong positive reaction or wanted to talk about my idea in much depth.

- 5: I've spoken with numerous people in my network who have validated this as a business need. Online market research has also validated there is a need.

- 10: I've talked to many people in my network. I've also talked to several target-business people. They seem very interested in this, have said it fills a gap, and are willing to pay for it—they see the return on investment. There is also a proven track record of people spending money in this area.

Time to Cash

How fast can you earn money?

- 1: Significant time and money investment is required up front. I can only earn back a percentage of the invested money this year.

- 5: Significant up front time or money is required, but I will be able to achieve positive cash flow within a couple of months with only a couple of customers.

- 10: Minimal startup capital is required. This is self-funding and can cash flow as soon as my first customer (from within my network) signs.

Sellable

Will you ultimately be able to sell this business (*can it make you rich*)?

- 1: No significant intellectual property, processes, or products will be created from this business. If I leave, the business falls apart.

- 5: A recurring revenue stream, minor product, and/or proprietary business processes will be created. I will capture some form of market share a competitor would benefit from buying.

- 10: Intellectual property will be created, ideally covered by patents. The business can operate and grow without me.

Score

On the far right, you'll see a score that is calculated by multiplying each column value together. The higher the score, the better the chance for fast success.

Phase 1 takeaways

Now that you have the columns filled out for a number of ideas, what thoughts and takeaways do you have? Do some of your ideas score strongly across the board?

Creating a successful business requires the right foundation. The points of evaluation in this phase help you understand the strength of your foundation. If you do not have an idea that jumps off of the page, take the time to find other ideas before moving on. Do so by talking to your network or reaching out to me at justin@justingesso.com.

Evaluator Phase 2: Customers

Phase 2 of business-idea evaluation looks at your customer base. Your customers will make or break you, so we need to know if the right customers are in your future.

> "There is only one boss. The customer. And he can fire everybody in the company from the chairman on down, simply by spending his money somewhere else."
> ~Sam Walton~

Spending big dollars on marketing and sales paves a risky, long road to building a business from scratch. But what if there's a better way? This portion of the 52x Business Evaluator is similar to Phase 1, but rather than evaluating your business ideas, you'll evaluate the strength of your network. When you rely on people within your network to grow your business, life is easy. You don't need to sell. You don't need to market. Your network does it for you.

Because I know this, I spend my time working on my network and relationships. It doesn't feel like selling to me. People get to know me, trust me, and understand what I do. If they need services I provide, using me is a no-brainer for them. Likewise, they gladly market my services on my behalf—often without even realizing it. Referrals of this nature are gold.

Forget pseudo science...this is how you make real magic happen.

My networking soapbox

Alright, I've spent a lot of time in this book harping on you to work your network. I'm going to make one more push here. While networking wasn't easy or natural for me, there are ways to approach it that work even for people like me and maybe you. If you haven't thrown yourself into genuinely improving your network, it's last-call time.

Consider this example of starting a marketing firm.

Scenario one

You know an executive at a midsize company. You have history. She understands your expertise and trusts you. She is the decision maker and actually needs to expand the company's marketing efforts, which so far have been minimal. As soon as you tell her you're starting a marketing firm, she asks to meet for lunch. You have an incredible discussion and together and create an exciting vision for their next-generation marketing.

You leave the lunch with a verbal agreement on a $60,000 engagement for the next three months. She goes back, gets the paperwork written up, and you're in business. Over time, your results come in, and the company decides to expand the engagement. You're hired on her staff. Your friend then gladly recommends you to peers in her network. Your business is ignited.

Scenario two

You "start" your business and spend a month building the perfect website, creating flyers, and getting all of your paperwork perfected. During month two, you "hit the streets," making phone calls and stopping by businesses. You find out most people aren't interested in the service you put together. After a lot of rejection, you realize people want something a little different.

You go back and spend the next few weeks changing your marketing and redoing your website. Month four, you hit the streets again and nail down one customer who is willing to do a $1,000 trial. You spend the next couple of weeks trying to get information and assets from them, only to realize it's taking all of your time and you're unable to focus on selling your next deal.

Dejected and broke, you decide this whole "small business" thing is too hard. Local business owners just don't have money and don't know what they really need.

Which scenario do you prefer?

In case you didn't know, this is how business actually plays out in the real world.

Let's think about it by answering these questions:

- Whom will you partner with?

- Who will beta test your products and services?
- Who will provide funding?
- Who will give you testimonials?
- Who will buy from your business?

The answer is people in your network. You need a strong network, and you need to double down on your efforts to improve it today.

Businesses versus consumers

Customers can be either individuals or businesses. Selling to either is perfectly viable. In the Phase 2 exercise, you'll see them referred to as:

- B2B: Business to Business (your business is selling to a business).
- B2C: Business to Consumer (your business is selling to a consumer).

The ranked factors in Phase 2 all apply, whether you are pitching to B2B, B2C, or some hybrid. If the questions don't apply perfectly to your customer type, adapt the spirit of the question to your scenario the best way possible.

 ## *Exercise* – Customer Evaluator (Phase 2)

The purpose of this phase is to target an initial set of customers to pitch to and work with for the concept of your offering (products or services). This scorecard will allow you to think through factors and rank accordingly. Once you've scored this phase of the Business Evaluator, you'll uncover the overlay between your business ideas and your network, allowing you to choose the right business for you.

Customer Name

Identify the specific person or group of people you'll sell to. Come up with at least 10 to evaluate. This could be "Jim" or "Real Estate Agents at XYZ Realty." People and groups are your rows.

Mapped Offerings

Which offering(s) of yours would this person/group be interested in? These are the offerings you listed in Phase 1.

Money

Rank this customer's ability to spend money. Does your customer already have a budget for what you're selling? If so, all you need to do is convince them to spend that budget on you. If not, you need to persuade them to create the budget and spend it on you. Go where the money is.

- 1: If B2B, they are a small, local business that sells low-dollar, low-margin items. They don't seem to do much marketing and aren't using the latest tech. If B2C, they are struggling with finances and unable to spend discretionarily.

- 5: This customer spends a good amount of money on things like advertising (B2B) or personal improvement (B2C). They have nice, updated items, such as offices, equipment, cars, and clothes.

- 10: This customer gets excited by new investments and ideas. They jump all in. They are growing, and everyone knows it. If B2B, I am good friends with the person who controls this money.

Influence

Rank your degree of influence and personal connection with this person from 1-10.

- 1: This customer doesn't see me as an expert in this area. I'm not very close with them.
- 5: This customer is aware of me and has an idea of my background. If I gave them some metrics and testimonials, I could convince them of my expertise, and I believe they'd listen to me.
- 10: This person already comes to me for advice. They know me, and they know my background. In fact, they should be paying me already.

Local

Rank this customer's accessibility to you.

- 1: They are out of state or the country. If B2B, they may have local presence, but the decision maker is not local; the people I'd work with are not all local either.
- 5: The people I'd work with are local, and they have strong influence over the decision maker.
- 10: The decision maker and operations people are local. Everyone I'd work with end-to-end is physically close, and I'd be able to spend time directly with them to tweak and improve my business.

Network

How well connected are you to the decision maker?

- 1: I do not know the decision maker, and I don't have someone who can readily introduce me.
- 5: I have a strong connection in my network who will introduce me to the decision maker.
- 10: I am very close with the decision maker.

Need

Does this customer need what you're offering?

- 1: They would need convincing to realize they need my offering.
- 5: It seems like they are aware my offering would help them, but they'd need to be convinced to spend money on it.
- 10: This customer realizes they need help in this area and are already spending money on it in one way or another. The budget and need are there for me already.

Growth

Is this customer growing? This is similar to the money rank but looks at the longer-term picture. Look at how this customer invests in their own improvement. Are they "going places," or do you see them stagnating for the next five years?

- 1: If B2B, this customer is falling behind in many ways, and I do not see them still being around in five years. Their office and equipment are outdated. The owner is participating in many operational aspects of the business.

If B2C, this customer will be in the same job or worse in five years.

- 5: This customer seems to be an up and comer. They are investing now to overtake existing competition and improve. If B2B, they are hiring. If B2C, they are improving themselves, are in shape, and are constantly seeking better employment.

- 10: If B2B, this customer dominates the market and are ensuring they stay there. They have a large marketing and sales budget. There are local economic factors that reinforce growth for their services in the foreseeable future. If B2C, this person is rapidly ascending, both professionally and personally. They are pursuing investments outside of work.

Customer evaluator takeaways

People are going to buy your product or service. Businesses fail because money doesn't come to them fast enough. People are the lubricant. When businesses fail, their owners talk about all sorts of technical reasons and causes. But what I see time and again is the right *people* were not in place: people were not adequately considered when the business idea was being formulated. When a business takes off, it's because of deep relationships in the right area. Don't underestimate the importance of this exercise and the impact it will have on your ability to make money quickly.

Do you have someone who will readily buy into your idea and make you profitable from day one? Or are you going to have to market, sell, chase down clients, and hustle for *months* before you see your first penny? If you are unable to leverage your network in your business startup, you may not be on the right playing field. Either look for another idea or invest the time to improve your network in the right areas.

Evaluator Phase 3: Competitors

Competitive analysis is a critical component to understanding how you must position yourself. I can almost guarantee you will have competition...and probably a lot of it. Competition alone should not stop you though. In fact, having others pave the path, create the audience, and make the mistakes can be very beneficial. Competitors can save you huge amounts of startup time and money. But, there are certain factors to watch out for. This phase will help you gather data, understand the landscape, and identify if any actual red flags exist.

> "It is nice to have valid competition; it pushes you to do better."
> ~Gianni Versace~

Some of the top excuses I hear from people who don't follow through on their ideas are:
- "It's already been done."
- "If only I did it first."
- "I could never compete with so-and-so. I don't have that kind of money, time, name, brand, resume, background, authority, funding, family, or whatever…"

While it's easy to stall due to competition, I have the opposite reaction, and so do the other successful business owners I know. Competition is exciting! Competition means:

- It can be done.

- Someone else has already made mistakes and adapted.

- I don't have to start from zero.

- I have a model to work from.

The fact that competition exists validates your business idea and gives you a place to start. If a competitor is doing well, that tells you it can be done!

You don't need to waste years learning your market or tweaking pricing. Instead of building an entire market from the ground up, your job simply involves hopping on the train, carving out a specialty, and doing just one thing better than the other guys.

Of course, some aspects of competition may invalidate your business idea, but if you did the "Customer" portion in the Business Evaluator and still made it this far, your idea has legs. Alright, head into the Phase 3 tab, and let's get rolling.

 ## Exercise – Competitor Evaluator

This phase is different than the first two. Whereas you ranked factors before, you will now take time to perform pointed research. The numbers you gather will help with the financial modeling coming up in Phase 4. The qualitative data will mature your perspective and shed light on valuable insights and opportunities.

For this research, I recommend utilizing your network first and the internet second. It's worth taking the time here to figure out how others are playing in your market. And if you can't find a company or person doing exactly what you're doing, find something similar. For example, maybe I want to sell an online course on making beer. I probably won't find much data on this topic specifically, but through an online search, I can get general information on selling online courses.

You will have to estimate as well. Use educated guesses, extrapolation, and ranges to figure these data points out as best as possible.

Pricing

How do your competitors make money? Is there fairly established pricing for what you plan to offer? Make sure to shop the major competitors. If you're offering a service, you may need to call them to do this research. How is pricing typically determined? Is it per hour, per project, per unit?

Units Sold

If you have the pricing and can determine their annual revenue or sales volume, then you can then estimate how many units they are actually moving using simple division. This is easier if the company is publicly traded, as the data will be readily available. But if not, research will likely turn up a CEO discussing their company size, sales figures, or some other data point that will clue you in.

Margin

Margin is the profit ratio. Of sales, how much money is that company keeping? If the company isn't publicly traded, you might need to do a bit more digging. Through a simple Internet search, you can also find typical profit margins based on industry and firm size.

Profit

Using the prior three columns, you should be able to calculate a rough profit estimate for this particular offering. This is calculated on the sheet for you.

Growth

By what percentage are your competitors growing? Again, this is much easier to determine if major players are publicly traded companies. You can look at their stock-price chart, look at shareholder reports, and find analyst views. You can also check sites such as LinkedIn, which will show company data on revenue and employee counts over the years.

As a last resort, you can use industry-growth numbers or the growth of some consumer-behavior indicator (e.g. "the demand for xyz services is expected to grow 37% over the next three years"). Try to get a year-over-year percentage growth.

If any company's growth is 20% or more, that indicates ample room for competitors to play.

On the other hand, negative growth is a sign of weakness. If most companies in this market are stagnant or shrinking, that is a sign of a tough market and prospect.

Locality

How many local companies exist in your town? Are they big? Do they advertise heavily? With moderate time and effort, can you stand out?

General Observations

As you do this research, be sure to jot down what the companies do and don't do well. Every company has its weaknesses, maybe because they're too big, too slow, and not responding to the market fast enough. Find opportunities to exploit, niches to carve, and areas to avoid. Maybe they're missing the needs of a key market audience. Also capture any best practices we can put in place at your business. I expect, during your research, you'll take *many* more notes than can fit here. Be sure to capture additional info in a notebook.

Competition red flags

While doing your research, if anything from the following list comes up, consider it a serious cause for concern. Unless you have a strong reason otherwise, I'd recommend scrapping the idea and moving on to the next (which should not be an issue thanks to your large idea list!).

Price Competition

A significant cause for concern is when companies in a particular area compete only on price. You want to be in a position where you're competing on value, features, and ability to deliver. Competing on price is a bad sign because it means that product or service has become a commodity. You will have a hard time standing out, and the winner will be determined by who has the cheapest and most efficient delivery chain. That's not where you want to play. Trying to grab customers here will be a major challenge.

Revenue Secondary

Similar to "price competition," another common situation companies get themselves into is providing their services for free to build a customer base now and hopefully sell later. The *hope* is to make money off of upsells, advertisements, or premium services. Think how many free online services you use. While this model can work (e.g. Google and Facebook), it takes a massive investment, and time-to-revenue can take a long time. If you want to start a business and profit this year, go where the money is now.

Bad Customers

Are you able to gain insight into these companies' customer base? This is especially possible if your business can be operated locally. Go back and look at the variables in Phase 2 of the Business Evaluator. How do your competitors' customers score? Do their potential customers have money, and are they happy to part with it in exchange for these services? If not, that's a red flag.

Decision point

Alright, you've done some research on your competitors and have been on the lookout for red flags. If you've uncovered red flags or other problems, you just need move on to the next idea. If, on the other hand, you don't see any red flags, then this is getting exciting! You will proceed to the next and final phase of the Business Evaluator. You also have keen insight into which models your business can follow and which opportunities you must exploit.

Evaluator Phase 4: Money

The last phase of the Business Evaluator checks to ensure you know how your business will make money and how much it can generate.

> "Businesses fail first and foremost because their ideas weren't sold quickly enough and in quantities great enough, and therefore they ran out of money."
> ~Grant Cardone~

As odd as it may sound, truly knowing how you will make money is a surprisingly overlooked facet of kicking off a business idea. I mean *really* knowing how you will make money—knowing how you will make money quickly; knowing who will give you the money; knowing the key variable to focus on to increase money; knowing the one activity to do every day to make money.

Remember, businesses fail because they don't make enough money fast enough. It's no more complicated than that. I hope you have an incredible business idea that you're passionate about. It's something that excites you. It creates massive value for your customers. It does much more for you and the world than just generatiE money. But guess what. If you don't have the money part figured out, your business idea will never blossom. It will never have the opportunity to add value to millions of people. It won't have the opportunity to change your life. You have to focus on the money. So let's do it!

Exercise – Money Evaluator

Head over to the last tab of the Business Evaluator. By now, you should have whittled down a list of 10+ business ideas to a select few. Here are some final items to look at:

Unit Name

What do you sell? What value are you adding to people? You need to specifically define this. Are you selling a book, a knowledge product, property management services, marketing services? If you're selling more than one product or service, list them on separate rows, but keep it to three or fewer. One of these products will probably make up 80%+ of your sales. I recommend focusing on just that one to start.

Price

How much do you charge for this product or service? You will test pricing in the future, but you should have a good placeholder idea for price thanks to the research you did in Phase 3. If you are offering a service, don't put an hourly price here—put a per-project price. For example, if you're starting a marketing-consulting service, don't focus on how much you'll charge people per hour: look at what you believe the average project will bring you. Again, use the 80% rule here to capture the most common scenario.

Monthly Units Sold

How many of those items will you sell per month? This is a number, along with price, that you can play with to model out different scenarios.

Monthly Expenses

What do you expect your monthly expenses to be? How much do you need to spend on office, technology, and advertising costs? Will you need human assistance? Humans are expensive! Attempt to estimate monthly expenses. A few tips:

- I recommend taking your estimated expenses and then multiplying the final number by somewhere between 1.5 and 2, depending on how confident you are. In other words, people generally estimate low, so add about 50% to 100% to your estimate.

- If you cannot reliably estimate your expenses, search the Internet for "profit margins by industry," or leverage your research from Phase 3. Searches such as this should return results on typical expenses and margins. You may need to dig a bit to understand where you'll fall in these ranges. Established companies likely have tons of overhead in terms of management, buildings, and more, but also have efficiencies of scale; regardless, it's a valuable benchmark and starting point for your projections.

Pre-Tax Profit

Alright, this is a simple calculation on the sheet. This is your profit minus your expenses. Nice! Play with "Price" and "Monthly Units Sold" to see how this number changes. For comparison's sake, when you take a job or receive a raise, you are thinking about *pre-tax* salary. So this number is the one most people think about when it comes to how much money they make.

Tax Rate

When you're a W-2 employee, it's easy to forget about taxes. They're magically pulled out of your paycheck every month. Running your own business is different. Handled properly, by running a business, you will likely pay *less* tax; however, you must be deliberate about tracking and paying it. To estimate a tax rate, do an Internet search for "business and individual tax rates." Better yet, contact a CPA, tell them what you're up to, and be confident about the number you put here. Most CPAs offer a free introductory hour session.

After-Tax Profit

Here's your final calculation. This is what actually goes in your pocket.

What's missing?

It's at this point that traditional business analysis would project into the future. That is, you estimate how sales and expenses change over time. You'd probably do a five-year projection. But, you might notice I include no time component in the 52x Business Evaluator. That's very intentional.

Typically, business cases estimate big expenses coupled with low sales volume at the start of a business. Other large expenses continue intermittently (perhaps moving to a bigger building, hiring management, investing in higher-volume machinery, etc...). Sales climb over time. And eventually, you may sell the company. That figure can also be calculated. This type of analysis produces year-over-year charts that look great on paper. You can also sum up the entire existence of the business into an IRR (internal rate of return) value. I've done this sort of analysis alongside other business experts countless times.

But...

...as I alluded to at the start of this chapter, I have yet to see it pan out. Before you launch and test a product, you are betting on how it will perform for years into the future. You are assuming you can reliably predict customer behavior, the competitive landscape, macro-economic events, and so much more.

I do not use this sort of view before launching a business or offering. Apart from being relatively futile, *it becomes an excuse for not making money now*!

If it looks like we may lose money this year, but I can project profit next year and massive millions of dollars in three years, well maybe I have the best business idea yet. And if it doesn't pan out, it wasn't my fault. Maybe we hired the wrong sales manager. Or, competitor XYZ just came out of nowhere. Projecting future profits is dangerous and full of unknowns. It's an excuse.

When is the future compelling?

While I'm driving to the point of "profiting now," there is a very compelling reason to think about the future—recurring revenue. If you sell something once, and it continues to bill on a monthly or other recurring basis, that is exciting. Go ahead and graph your growing sales volume over time. It can really be amazing.

However, I want to caution you not to lean on this as a crutch. Just like any other outlook modeling, the further out you go, the more unknowns you have. I hope recurring profit makes you rich, but don't rely on it to make profit now.

Lastly, the more secure you are financially and business wise, the more risk you can afford to take. If you have great income and successful businesses under your belt, you may be willing to take on the risk involved in a long-term business case. You may be just fine spending a large amount of money and years of work to have a huge payoff five years from now. But for most of us, stick to that which doesn't rely on multi-year projections.

No excuses—profit now

I'm going to emphasize this one more time:businesses fail because they don't make enough money fast enough. Period. I want you to succeed. I want you profit now.

Don't let future profits justify a business. Before you know it, you'll be six months down the line hanging out with your justifications and excuses:

Just six more months...

As soon as we get this new version launched…

We're trying something new to improve conversion rates...

To profit now, we need to be *now* oriented. And we need to focus on what you can control *now*. And in fact, there are some ways we can evaluate the numbers from a *now* orientation. Here are some questions to get you thinking:

- Go back into the spreadsheet and play with the numbers, particularly "units sold." How many units do you need to sell each month to be profitable?

- What happens if you double that number?
- Does that sales quantity seem reasonable?
- What tasks and activities can you start immediately to begin hitting those numbers?

Business Evaluation Conclusion

Alright, this was Phase 4 of your business evaluation. You've looked at your offering, your customers, your competitors, and the details of your money. A single business idea should have bubbled to the top. It shows terrific promise across all four phases. You should have great clarity into why it will succeed and what you need to do in order to make that happen.

The next chapter will take you through a final verification of the key points in this entire evaluation process, so you should be feeling very strongly about your business idea right now. If, on the other hand, you're still struggling or these exercises haven't helped clarify whether or not your business is based on a successful foundation, please contact me at justin@justingesso.com.

Assuming you have selected a rockstar idea, move forward, and let's change your life!

CHAPTER 10

Final Preparation

Goals

- We're here. It's time to make the last checks before picking your business.
- Get to the heart of what will make your business a success...what you can control.
- Begin orienting your future activities around your commitment.
- Ensure you are continuing the right practices and habits.
- Validate you are really ready to start your business.
- **Action:** Use the daily and monthly worksheets at *justingesso.com/52x*
- **Action:** Take at least one big daily action toward each of your Grinder-3 Goals

Business-Selection Checklist

We just completed the 52x Business Evaluator, but we covered a lot of ground, so let's perform a couple more checks to ensure nothing fell through the cracks. We also need to ensure you know how your business will make money and that you know the single variable that will determine how much it will generate. This will be your "Business-Selection Checklist."

> "A checkride ought to be like a skirt, short enough to be interesting but still be long enough to cover everything."
> ~Aviation Wisdom from Unknown Source~

We'll also close Part III with a "Pre-Flight Checklist" that will review your progress from Parts I, II, and III of this book. Burying your head in the detailed analysis of a business idea can cause you to lose sight of the bigger picture. So let's ensure all of your personal fundamentals are still in place, setting you up for the best launch possible.

 ## Exercise – Business-Selection Checklist

Alright, here you are—standing outside of your new business. You've done a ton of introspection and work to get here. Your business is ready for you to hop in and start it up. Are you ready?

Run through these questions and make sure you can respond with a resounding YES to each.

Offering Checklist

Does your business idea:

- Excite you?
- Allow you to sell face-to-face locally, even if you plan on going global?
- Solve a problem for people who are ready to buy your service/product?

Customer Evaluator

Do your potential customers:

- Have enough money to liberally spend on your offering?
- Have decision making authority?
- Trust you to deliver?
- Have local operations you can visit?
- Have strong growth?

Competitors Checklist

Do your competitors:

- Provide a success model you can follow?
- Compete on value instead of price?
- Charge for all of their services as opposed to attracting customers with free services?
- Have the type of customers that score well on the Customer Evaluator?

Money Checklist

Does your business:

- Have a specific unit you will sell?
- Have a path to make profit immediately?

Stop!

Did you pass? If so, awesome...time to climb in and start that shiny new business up.

If not, spend more time working on ideas. If you're stuck on a particular aspect of the Business Evaluator, contact me at justin@justingesso.com, and let's work through it.

The One Thing

As you work the Business Evaluator all the way down through the checklist, you will uncover that once you have a good idea with the right fundamentals, there is *one thing* that will determine your success—the number of units you sell. The secret sauce behind any great business is sales. End of story.

Through the 52x Business Evaluator, we've determined your business has potential. You have no excuses for failure...except *your* ability to sell. And for you to be able to sell, you must be obsessed with your idea. You must be contagiously enthusiastic. You must hustle.

If your idea checks out on paper, you need to ask yourself if you are sold on the idea. *Are you sold*?

If you're not completely, undeniably, absolutely obsessed and 100% sold on your business, no one else will be either. People won't buy your product. Your marketing copy won't inspire conversation. People won't want to come work for you. Though it's a great idea, your business will flop.

Just because your business idea checks out on paper and withstands the evaluation test doesn't mean it will be a success. You must be personally sold on it.

Sell yourself, and the business will take care of itself

Knowing "the one thing" that determines your success up front allows you to build a massively successful business. Why? If you ask yourself if you're *sold* at every step of the way, you will build quality into your service or product. You will have something you're proud of...end-to-end. You will be so sold, you won't even feel like you're *selling* when you're selling.

This is also how you'll beat your competitors. No matter how tough they may seem, you can be more sold on your product. Because you're sold, you will sell to others better. You will go further. You'll push harder. You'll make it happen and exhaust your competitors.

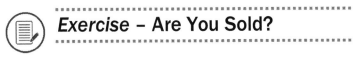

Exercise – Are You Sold?

The one thing that will determine your success is sales. Are you sold on your idea? In the white space on this page, write the word YES!

Pre-Flight Checklist

From here forward, you will be focusing on building your business, executing, and profiting. To this point, you've learned a lot, done a lot, and packed in a lot of habits. Let's make sure everything has come together properly and nothing has fallen through the cracks.

> "Your net worth to the world is usually determined by what remains after your bad habits are subtracted from your good ones."
> ~Benjamin Franklin~

Exercise – Pre-Flight Checklist

Here we go! You've done some major introspection, put ideas through rigorous evaluation, and are sitting at the cusp. For some of you, the concept of starting your business may be "too real" at this point, and you will turn away. But I believe if you've made it this far and you've aligned your business idea with your personal drivers, you should be unbelievably excited. Your idea has wings. You're about to do something that will completely change your life. You will enjoy your work, make massive amounts of money, and build your legacy.

If you have concerns about your answers to these checklist items, it is likely worth pausing and taking the time to make the adjustments needed before going forward. If, however, you sail through this checklist with nothing but resounding YES answers, then the only thing left is to let loose and fly.

Question 1

Do I know my personal Mission Statement, and do I write it down at least once per week?

- Yes
- Not yet

Question 2

Am I finding ways to keep myself motivated and energized? For example, do I listen to audio books whenever I have a chance...and particularly during commutes? Do I understand that motivation is more critical now than earlier in the program?

- Yes
- Not yet

Question 3

Am I actively using a tool, such as Habitica, to gamify and make habit tracking enjoyable? At this point, have I filled this system with habits and tasks such as: reading self-advertisements, writing down goals, and calling people in my network? Does this compliment my written to-do system?

- Yes
- Not yet

Question 4

Do I handwrite my Grinder-3 Goals at on my *52x Daily Tracker*? At this point, do I have them memorized? Am I excited to achieve them? Am I getting closer to achieving them?

- Yes
- Not yet

Question 5

Do I have a system in place to track my contacts, and do I update it at least once per week? Am I actually calling at least 10 (hopefully more) people each week in order to develop and nurture my network? Do I have a calendar reminder or habit established to ensure this gets done?

- Yes
- Not yet

Question 6

Have I begun the exercise of completing the *52x Money Master* worksheet? Do I have a habit or calendar item in place to ensure I complete it once per month? Even if I don't have business income, do I understand the value of getting into the habit and mindset? Do I know my projected year-end income and how far off of target I am if I don't make changes?

- Yes
- Not yet

Question 7

Have I established my one, three, five, and 10 year master plan? Do I know where I want to go in life? While I understand this will evolve over time, do I know it serves as a strong guidepost for my actions today? Am I thinking 52x?

- Yes
- Not yet

Question 8

Have I crafted at least 20 self-advertisements? Have I hand-written them on note cards, and am I reviewing these note cards at least once per day? Do these affirmations directly tackle my points of friction and excite me about achieving my goals?

- Yes
- Not yet

Question 9

Each and every day, am I taking at least one action (to-do) on each of my Grinder-3 Goals?

- Yes
- Not yet

Question 10

Am I taking the exercises in this book seriously? Am I spending time on crafting personal and well-thought-out answers? Am I not rushing or short-changing myself? Do I understand the value is there, but only if I give it my all?

- Yes
- Not yet

Question 11

Have I freed up or found time every day to commit to building my business on the side or full time? Whether in my personal or business life, have I reduced my workload by stopping, automating, and outsourcing? Do I apply this filter to everything new that comes my way, and do I have a much more streamlined approach to time?

- Yes
- Not yet

Question 12

Do I know where my money comes from, and do I budget my time accordingly? Have I stopped spending excess time on low-value activities?

- Yes
- Not yet

Question 13

Am I obsessed with my goals, my mission, and my business idea? Do I literally go to sleep thinking about my future, and do I wake up early, excited about it? Do I know being obsessed about my idea is what will make it happen and what will allow me to slaughter the competition?

- Yes
- Not yet

Question 14

If I am in a low-growth situation, do I understand the cards are stacked against me? Do I know growth is critical to supporting the goal of launching a successful business? Do I understand this may mean I need make a big change, such as building a new people network or moving to a another city?

- Yes
- Not yet

Question 15

Without a healthy body, do I know I am not optimized as a human and will not reach my potential? Am I eating well and keeping my body moving?

- Yes
- Not yet

Question 16

Have I created a list of what scares me—my anti-goals? Any time I waiver or lose motivation, do I flip back to that section in my notebook and review why I'm doing this? Are my anti-goals strong enough that they immediately restore my focus, motivation, and obsession? Do I know exactly what the heck I'm fighting for?

- Yes
- Not yet

Question 17

Have I passed my engines start checklist, successfully vetting my business idea?

- Yes
- Not yet

Question 18

If I'm struggling with ANYTHING in this book, do I ensure it doesn't deter me?! Do I ask for help, input, and support from my spouse, friends, or network? Do I also not hesitate to email justin@justingesso.com or find another way to get the support I need to move forward and do an awesome job? Do I understand these exercises, when done properly, are challenging and that many of my best ideas will come from interacting with others?

- Yes
- Not yet

Part IV

Launch

Part IV Introduction

Many self-help and motivational books would stop after Part III. But I feel a duty to carry on. Hopefully, you've built up a tremendous amount of momentum and are ready to actually pull the trigger on a great business idea containing strong potential. But taking that actual first step can be daunting—so daunting, in fact, that most people will get to this point and never actually take that step. Let's make sure you're one of the few.

CHAPTER 11

Action Plan

Goals

- Define your business commitment.
- Break down your goals
- Organize your actions
- Determine the best way to get help with vendors and employees
- Decide if you will achieve more by partnering
- Take constant action
- **Action:** Use the daily and monthly worksheets at *justingesso.com/52x*
- **Action:** Take at least one big daily action toward each of your Grinder-3 Goals

Business Commitment

We started this book by defining your personal mission statement. Now that we stand at the cusp of your business launch, it's time to do the same for it. I have a somewhat unique take on business mission statements. I want a declaration—a commitment—that you can and will shout out to your customers every chance you get.

This business commitment should help make it clear to you and everyone else exactly what your business does.

> **"Just as people cannot live without eating, so a business cannot live without profits. But most people don't live to eat, and neither must businesses live just to make profits."**
> ~John Mackey, Whole Foods~

Your business will become a vehicle for achieving *your* personal mission. Businesses allow you to reach people by scaling. You can add value to many, and through this, realize not only profit, but also a higher purpose. By aligning your personal mission statement with your business one, you will become even more sold on your success. And since everything hinges on you being sold, this is important.

A *business commitment* is the best way to verbalize the mission of your business to everyone. Whereas a mission statement can go on conference room walls, a *commitment* is much broader reaching. Simply put, you need to define what your business is committed to doing for your customer.

 ## *Exercise* – Business Commitment

Writing a commitment forces you to precisely identify your service/product, who your target market is, and how your service/product adds value to their lives. So let's get started by answering these questions:

- What do you sell?

- Whom do you sell it to?
- How does it improve the lives of people who buy it? Said another way, what problem does it solve for people?
- How is your solution unique?

Now, put these answers together in the form of one or two concise sentences. The commitment starts with "I am committed to...," or a variation of that.

To give you an example, you can look at this book's commitment. It is simple and descriptive: "My commitment is to help you start a business and profit this year."

Once you have your statement drafted, go back and compare it to your personal mission statement. Do they jive? Can you extract concepts and emotions from your personal mission statement to spice up your business commitment?

Grab your notebook and write down your business commitment. This commitment will ultimately be on your website, in your marketing, and everywhere a potential customer may see it.

It's also very important that you share this statement with trusted people in your network and get their feedback. Does it excite them? Do they understand it properly? Does it get them jazzed up to become a beta customer?

Ideas into Action

It can be easy to become motivated by big ideas and big goals. But if you don't know how to start, that enthusiasm can quickly wane and turn into frustration, or worse...nothing. Breaking a goal down to something you can take action on without even thinking allows you to carry motivation into daily action. This is how you see big stuff through. If you ever find yourself stuck, you likely just need to break down your next steps even further.

> "Nothing is particularly hard if you divide it into small jobs"
> ~Henry Ford~

Taking action is all about starting with the end in mind and brainstorming backward to where you are right now. You identify the actionable chunks that come up along the way. "Actionable" is the key word. You need to settle on tasks that are small enough that they can be easily conceptualized and completed within a day or two. You want to transition from some high-in-the-clouds goal to a step you can take right now.

Here's an example of how to go from a specific goal to a daily action:

- **Goal:** In my first year of my small business, I want to net $400,000.
- I did the math and discovered I need 100 customers to make this happen.
- Based on research, I expect I will have a 2% conversion rate (2% of the people I talk to will buy my product).
- That means I need to talk to 5,000 people this year.
- That breaks down to 19 people per day.
- **Daily Action:** I need to talk to 19 people about my business every day.

- **Secondary Action:** Find ways to improve that 2% conversion rate.

Good news: talking to 19 people per day is nothing to generate that sort of money. That's three hours of work. That still leaves many more hours every day to work on your business and delivery. And what if you don't want to make all of those 19 calls? You can ultimately hire a commission-based salesperson. Run your numbers again to cover the cost and set the salesperson's daily call goal appropriately.

This approach allows you to avoid overcomplicating business problems. Figure out what you want, uncover the driving variable, and then press through it daily.

Other tasks and actions related to starting your business are going to be much more task oriented. Mind maps tackle this problem beautifully.

Exercise – Create a Mind Map

As of now, you have your end in mind. You have a business idea supported by your personal goals. Now we want to uncover which steps you need to take in order to make your business idea a reality. I recommend doing this by using mind-mapping techniques. Here's how to get started.

In the middle of a page, write down your business idea. Around it, start writing out all of the things needed to make that idea happen. Connect those ideas back to your main business idea with a line. These items are still likely very big in scope and not yet actionable. So, pick one of them and start breaking it down into further chunks, continuing to draw lines back to each parent level.

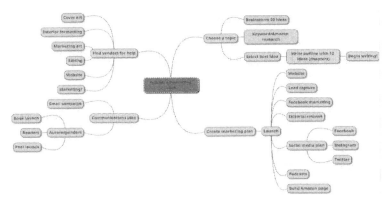

As you break down your business idea, you need to keep going until you arrive at tasks that are small and relatable. Typically this means you've broken them down into tasks you can accomplish within one day.

And don't worry—if you're not quite sure yet which actions you need to take, I'll give you plenty in the upcoming chapter. But it's important to nail down this concept first and get started with the actions you know.

Before you move on, build out as much of a mind map about your business idea as possible. You can use a simple sheet of paper, or you can head to *mindmup.com* for a free mind-mapping tool.

Organizing Actions

Through the previous exercise, you started building a mind map full of tangible items you can chase after. The next step is to take those actions and turn them into a checklist. The goal is to be able to wake up, look at a list, pick something to do, and go. This is how you eliminate worry and doubt. This is how you'll eliminate confusion and wasted time. This approach delivers simplicity. It's time to get stuff done.

And talk about getting obsessed—this approach gives you exactly what you need to focus on daily. As you see your big goals start breaking down under your pressure, your excitement and focus will explode...as will your productivity and results.

Grab your mind map, take the bubbles that are furthest out, (the furthest breakdown of your goals and actions) and write them down in a list. I recommend you take a couple of approaches with this list:

If you're a visual person, create an action board

Physically write all of the furthest mind-map breakdown actions on paper. Use graph paper, colored paper, or whatever gets you excited. Now, cut each action out so it becomes its own little sheet. Take these actions and pin them on cork board and hang it on your wall.

As you complete these items, pull them off the board and put them in a victory jar. See your victory jar fill up, and watch your action board vanish. It's an awesome approach to starting a business.

If you're a tech-oriented person, get in the cloud

If you're not the type to put something like this in your office, find an online tool that serves a similar purpose. Personally, I use *Trello*. It's free and allows you to create an online version of the action board. You can organize your actions into different groups. Make sure to create a "Victory" List (a List is a column containing a group of Cards) into which you can move your completed items.

You'll get the same sense of progress, and you'll see this mass array of actions whittled down in no time.

Exercise – Just Start Working

There's a jarring change that occurs between finding an idea and executing it. This chapter is about making it over that hurdle. Once you've broken down your actions and prioritized them, it's simply time to get to work. The days of being lost in thought, introspection, and analysis now need to give way to practical motion.

> "Amateurs sit and wait for inspiration, the rest of us just get up and go to work."
> ~Stephen King~

This motion and hard work can be equally satisfying. And, it's what separates the dreamers from the doers. If you want your idea to materialize, you need to make the mental shift and start working through your list.

Some people tackle this by forcing themselves to work on these items uninterrupted for a certain period of time every day. Many authors force themselves to write a certain number of words per day. Though I'm largely in control of my time, when I hit this stage, I typically wake up around 4 a.m. and get this work done in the distraction-free quiet I only find in the early mornings. People take these measures because it is not easy to just start working. Find your way.

Vendors and Employees

Within your large action list, there will undoubtedly be items that you can't or don't want to do. Certain actions will be best handled by someone else. Other people will need to be responsible for building and growing your business. Avoiding help is a huge mistake and will hold you back.

The good news is there are a variety of ways you can accelerate your business processes without breaking the bank. The bad news is people are complicated...and employees even moreso. Here are some common ways to get help and knock your action lists out quickly and efficiently.

Freelancer marketplaces

For one-off tasks such as logo design, utilize global-vendor marketplaces such as *Fiverr.com* or *Upwork.com*. These types of sites get you in touch with skilled freelancers from across the globe, allowing you to have work completed for as little as $5. This sort of engagement is especially useful when you are first building your company or brand. It allows you to build a professional image for your material while keeping costs down.

Interns

If you have ongoing part-time work, interns can be great. I generally have one intern assisting me at any given time. With internships, you can find skilled and motivated people who will work for free or a small amount. In exchange, you will need to provide real experience in their field, including training, and mentoring. You'll probably need to fill out paperwork as you go.

Additionally, internships are usually temporary, so there is some time lost in continually retraining new interns.

Remember, interns are looking to build experience that will help them land a full-time job after they graduate. You should have a genuine interest in supporting them accordingly. By doing this, our interns typically end up extending their internship and staying for a long time, which is an added bonus and lessens the retraining burden.

Interns can be great for a variety of tasks, but I've most commonly utilized them for technical help, social media, research, content creation, outreach, search engine optimization, public relations, and marketing assistance.

If you have a university or college near your town, great. You simply need to contact the school, fill out some paperwork, and then post your internship. I live in a university town, which broadens my selection pool. Most cities at least have a college nearby.

If not, you can submit an internship to national posting boards and gain help remotely. I haven't personally used these but do know several people who rely heavily on them. Examples include *internships.com* and *internjobs.com*.

As a last note, you can build a team of interns and have one of your longer-term interns take over the onboarding and training of newer interns. This "master intern" should be someone on a management track who is looking to build such experience. You will still need to be involved with everyone, but this can reduce your overhead and provide more of a career path for the master intern.

Virtual assistants

Similar to interns, you can hire virtual assistants (VA) to provide as-needed services on an ongoing basis. These people are typically located in lower-cost regions and have certain specializations. Since you may need to share personal details and data with your VA, trust and security are important.

There are a variety of ways to find a good VA, but the only way to go, in my opinion, is to get a personal recommendation from someone in your network. Failing that, you can post to virtual assistant job boards or contact a company that specializes in virtual assistance. By going direct, you can save quite a bit of money but will have more risk when it comes to skills, timeliness, security, and results. If you go with a VA company, you can alleviate most of these concerns and enjoy a systematized approach to work assignment. However, these companies can end up being expensive.

Ideally, you find someone you trust, enjoy working with, and can grow over time. I greatly enjoy working with people overseas and have done so most of my career. Just like with hiring U.S. employees, you'll have good and bad experiences. Don't write off VAs because of one person.

Contractors

If you need regular, ongoing assistance from someone with a specific skillset, you'll need to consider whether you hire them as a contractor or regular employee. Contractors present lower risk for companies and allow more flexibility in regard to engagement length.

Let's say you need assistance building and maintaining your website and online marketing. You could hire an employee to do this. But what if you have a lot of upfront work and only a couple of hours per week ongoing? What if you don't like the quality of the employee's work and want to change who you're using? What if you don't know how to instruct and guide the employee?

Anyone can be a contractor. You don't need to hire some marketing company to fulfill your website and online marketing needs. Reach out to your network and see if there is anyone who can give you what you need on the side. You pay them as a contractor, and life is great.

Contractors can be very similar to employees. If you've worked at a large corporation, you almost certainly have contractors working for the company 40 hours per week. They have a company email address, a company badge, and may do the same work as you.

So what's the difference? It's all about who controls the work. Employees can be instructed precisely what to do, when, and how. Contractors are instead given a deliverable and timeframe. They are expected to produce some result by some date. They are then allowed to direct themselves as they see fit.

As an owner, working with contractors is much simpler than working with an employee. Contractors invoice you at the end of the month, and you pay them. You will submit a tax document at the end of the year so the contractor can pay taxes appropriately, but that's about it in terms of overhead. Taxes are handled via a 1099 form, which is why you often hear them referred to as "1099 contractors."

With all of these benefits, some companies end up using contractors when they are really acting as employees. This is a problem and can get you into trouble. Since every situation is unique, be sure to review IRS information (search *IRS.gov for "independent contractor or employee*) on this topic as you consider bringing on a 1099 contractor...and again as the working relationship matures over time.

Employees

I started this section by saying *people* are key to building and growing your businesses. Going it alone will hold you back. If you've exhausted the alternatives above and you need help, do yourself a favor and hire an employee. Sure, they bring risk and overhead into your business, but they can also help take you to the next level.

If you had someone handling your administrative tasks or delivering your services, could you free up time to sell and network more? Yes! You should constantly strive to work on high-value tasks while pushing lower-value tasks downstream. You focus on the levers that drive money and leave the rest to your team.

When you first decide to hire an employee, you will likely need to talk to accountant and possibly an attorney. This will ensure you have the right forms, processes, insurance, and tax handling to manage an employee. You'll also want to review human resources best practices to give your employee the support structure they need and to give you a paperwork trail in case something goes wrong.

In terms of cost, you don't just pay a salary. You pay taxes, unemployment, vacation, breaks, and potentially other costs, such as benefits. The fully-loaded cost of an employee is typically 1.2 to 1.5 times their salary. So if you pay someone $40,000 per year, you should plan on actual costs of $60,000.

And as with everything I recommend, rely on your network to find a great employee. Employees are a big commitment. The relationship can be very intense, so it is critical to put in the effort to find the right person. There is only so much a resume and interview can tell you about someone. Exhaust recommendations from your network before posting on job boards.

Partnerships are your secret weapon

If you need high-level help to grow your business and want to pay for this on a percentage (margin) basis rather than as an expense, you are better off partnering with the right person. This one is so huge I have devoted the entire next section to it. So, keep reading.

Getting your money's worth from people

Since I want you to be profitable from Day 1, it's very important to apply return-on-investment criteria to people. They need to result in business growth, not expense. As an example, let's say you're a real estate agent considering hiring a transaction coordinator to handle your paperwork. You're doing this because you want to transition from being a real-estate agent to being a proper business person.

If you make $100,000 today, and the coordinator will cost you $35,000 per year, how do you justify that cost?

Simple. You need to sell more houses. That person must free up enough time for you to earn an extra $5,000 per month, or $60,000 per year. For most agents, that's one sale per month. If you hired someone to handle your paperwork, marketing, and non-client communication, could you achieve one extra sale per month? You better. Figure out how many more calls you must make to generate one extra sale per month. Will a coordinator free up that time or more for you? If so, do it.

But what if you can have employees generate revenue too?

In our real estate business, all but one of our assistants have their real estate license. They work 20-35 hours per week as an employee and pursue selling real estate on their own time. We then keep a percentage of each sale they make. It's a win-win. They are able to make as much money as their ambition allows (sales) but also have a steady base (the W-2 work). Thanks to the percentage we earn, these employees pay for themselves and then some. In other words, the money we keep from their sales exceeds their payroll expense. We have a large team that gets it done and costs us virtually nothing

In another business, we ensure a portion of the new hire's can be billed directly to a client. Similar to the above example, perhaps 20 hours of the person's work is for our company, and the other 20 is billed out to a client engagement. This allows us to add employees and grow the company at little to no expense.

The point of this section is to be creative in your approach to adding people. You will need people if you want to grow, so find ways to do it that won't sink your ship.

Exercise – Have fun and offload!

Once you decide to get help, start delegating! Go back to your to-do list and mind-map actions. Here's what you should delegate:

- Everything you've been procrastinating
- Everything you don't know how to do (let someone else handle the research)
- Everything you do poorly
- Non-value-add work
- Things that don't result in more money

Now for the ultimate way to get highly-skilled help...

Partnerships

While reading this chapter, you must have been asking yourself: *Can I really successfully pull off this business? Or, am I holding myself back?* People are almost always the largest cost a business sees, but missing revenue or never starting is unacceptable. Don't let the need for help block you. A partnership may be just the answer you need.

> "Great things in business are never done by one person. They are done by a team of people."
> ~Steve Jobs~

You can't penny-pinch your way to millions. But you can be smart about how you invest in your business. Partnerships are just such a way to do so.

I've pursued certain ventures on my own, but I pursue most with a partner. I've always been a "do-all-it-yourself" sort of guy, and I suspect many people who want their own business are too. But as I've built more experience, I value the benefits of partnerships more and more. Great partnerships offer the chance for more money, more success, and more personal growth. This section will help you determine if a partnership is right for you.

The Big-4 skills

To run a great business that generates money, four high-level skills are critical. Here are the Big 4:

- Creative
- Sales
- Marketing
- Technical

If you're missing very strong skills in any of these areas, you will have a hard time launching a successful business. There are, of course, many other areas to consider depending on your business type, but these skills relate specifically to being able to offer and sell your product. Here's a deeper dive on each:

- **Creative** is the skill of generating business ideas that meet consumer demand. This is the skill that allows you to come up with business ideas, find ways to deliver those ideas to customers, and adapt to changes in the market.
- **Sales** is the ability to effectively convey the value of a product or service such that customers gladly exchange

their money for it. This is a one-on-one and one-on-many skill. It spans in-person communication and sales copy that appears in print on your website, in marketing material, and more.

- **Marketing** is a statistics- and data-oriented skill focused on branding and lead generation. It also includes the discipline of launching products and services, managing their lifecycle, and gathering market feedback.

- **Technical** is the set of skills required to make your product or service deliverable to customers. Somehow, orders from your business must be fulfilled. Whether this is via website orders or in-person ones at a store, you need skills to set up the business functionality (from marketing to delivery). This could also be called "Operations," but more and more, this is about automating and integrating systems, which is why I term it "Technical."

Do you have a gap in one of these Big 4? This is very commonly the case. In fact, I have frequently seen business owners have the first two or last two skills from this list. But it's rare I see someone with true depth in all four.

In order to address any gaps you have, there are three options:

- Build your skills
- Hire someone to fill the gaps
- Partner with someone to fill the gaps

Over time, you will undoubtedly build your skills, but will this happen fast enough? Will you have the time and interest to do so? Often, a strong salesperson and visionary could do portions of the marketing but simply isn't interested or won't do a complete job. If you spend time chasing down one of these skills, will your business suffer while you do?

The second options is to hire someone to fill gaps. The problem here is you will quickly find that filling any of the top-level skill gaps with good people is expensive...I mean *really expensive.*

People who have true strengths in the Big 4 are in demand. That skillset is required to run businesses successfully, and the market recognizes this. Additionally, none of these areas are one-time engagements. Sure, you can pay someone a flat fee to create a website for you—but the reality is, you will need to constantly tweak, adjust, and enhance your entire online platform. Each of these skill areas require ongoing attention.

Your third option is a partnership with someone who has aspirations like you. You bring your idea and show them your work in the 52x Business Evaluator. You're sold on it, so you sell them on it too. They've been yearning to do something big...but just didn't know what. You brought them just what they needed: an idea and a motivated partner.

Partnership example

Let's say you have a very unique investing strategy and want to create an online course to teach it. You are excited to write the content and create videos. You are enthusiastic and can sell the idea to anyone you talk to. You have the first two skills (creative and sales) down.

But, you're not the type to figure out how to create an entire online system to actually deliver and sell this course. Further, the more you look into online marketing, the more you realize how sophisticated it really is. You talked to a few people and realized hiring an agency to do this is insanely expensive...and can you really trust them? Perhaps you try and don't really get the results you want.

But what if, thanks to your habit of making networking calls every week, you find someone in your network who has these skills. She's been wanting to start her own business but doesn't really have an idea or the desire to write content and sell. She's looking to break into the business of designing online platforms and doing marketing but doesn't have a portfolio yet. She's trustworthy. She's willing to put it on the line and make your idea happen...and she doesn't get paid unless you do.

In this example, your interests are directly aligned with her interests. You both make money when the same goal is achieved. You both have intrinsic value to gain. This sort of scenario is commonplace and is how I've grown most of the businesses I'm involved in.

In fact, this example is pretty close to a real-life partnership of mine. I was the "she" here and brought the technical and marketing skills. The original owner had a very high-quality product. He was great at live discussions and could sell in person beautifully. But he struggled with gaining any traction online. He spent a lot of money on a local marketing agency but was unable to consistently sell online.

After partnering, we began getting things off the ground. We both learned from each other. Ultimately, we grew the business by 700% pretty rapidly, and it's still growing. We're both making much more money than if we hadn't partnered. The partnership is also the source of other benefits, including building our "Big 4" skills, growing our personal networks, and motivating us to expand into other projects.

What is a partnership?

A partnership is "A legal form of business operation between two or more individuals who share management and profits." I'm not going to dive into that definition any further, nor will I cover the various legal types of partnerships; that would be boring...and that's what attorneys are for. Rather, I want to dive into three key words in that definition: share, management, and profits.

Share

It's important to note that you don't need to share management and profits 50/50. I intentionally put the topic of "partnerships" after choosing a business idea because I want you to be the primary owner. I want you to have more than a 50% stake— and more than 50% of the profit. But if you need help, don't fail during the launch. Share in the profits, and you will likely make orders of magnitude more than you would alone.

Management

When you write up your partnership agreement, you'll decide how decisions are made, but at the end of the day, the majority holder typically has the majority vote. I like to retain this ultimate control, but the reality is, if you have a great working relationship with your partner, you will compliment each other and come up with much better decisions than if either of you had gone it alone.

If you must constantly rely on an agreement to override partners, you might not have the right partners.

Profits

After having read the first sections of this book, I hope you've decided to pursue this business for much more than money. And, I hope your partner has much more to gain from this venture than just the profits. But, money is all powerful, so it's good to know how this works. In a partnership, you need to split the profits (typically in accordance with the same percentage as the management vote). Profits come after expenses, so it may be months before you profit. Because of this, you also need to consider costs—particularly big capital costs—up front. If you have a 10% partner, are you expecting them to pay 10% of that big five-year web hosting expense?

Bringing the three partnership factors together

You'll need to spend time thinking through the three factors just described. I recommend discussing them with your prospective partner, coming to your own idea of how things should run and then putting your ideas on paper. Once you've come to an agreement, attorneys or online legal-document services can help you consider additional questions and scenarios. Then, formalize the agreement.

Legal framework aside, a partnership is about aligning interests, completing skillsets, and building your leadership team without spending upfront money (remember that *profit-now* thing?). Done properly, a partnership can set you both up to make residual, passive income for the rest of your life. Partnerships will get you places you never expected to go. They are perhaps the best tool available to people starting a small business.

With whom do you partner?

A business relationship is, in fact, very intense by nature, so you need to be able to get along with people, and you need to find someone you know you can get go through ups and downs with. This means you must know the person very well. Does this mean you should partner with a friend?

While partnering with a friend might not always work out, you do know your friends and have a solid understanding of how they operate. You should have a good idea of whether or not the relationship will work. You likely have some history together that will transcend minor issues and disagreements. Personally, all of my partners are also friends, and I wouldn't have it any other way.

Friend or otherwise, here are some criteria to review when considering a prospective partner:

- Are they trustworthy?
- Do they have goals like yours?
- Are their values similar?
- Do they have more to gain from this partnership than just money?
- Do their "Big 4" skills complement yours (creative, sales, marketing, technical)?
- Is this someone I can learn from?
- Do we brainstorm well together?
- What's their level of dedication?

What if you don't know someone who meets these criteria? Network! If you don't have someone you trust, you need to find a strong referral through your network. Partnerships are not something for which you can post a "help wanted" ad.

Finding a referral through your network may take a bit more vetting. As you talk to this referral, spend time getting to know them up front. Consider paying them as a contractor initially to get a sense of their style, work ethic, and personality. If things work out and you have synergy with them, you can then move to a partnership level.

Money, taxes, and liability

The first concern I hear almost everyone bring up about partnerships is the paperwork and added complexity. Look, even if you operate as an individual, you need to deal with these issues, and you still should engage a CPA and an attorney. So if having a partner will help your business be massively more successful, then don't let administrative paperwork stop you...you're going to have it regardless.

 ## Exercise – Is a Partnership for You?

If the concept of partnering resonates with you, this may be the idea that opens up your potential. If you answer "yes" to any of the questions below, get partnering.

Question 1

Am I missing one of the "Big 4" skills (creative, sales, marketing, technical)?

- Yes
- No

Question 2

Am I unable to pay the salaries needed to help launch my business successfully (including the critical times early on when your business isn't yet profitable)?

- Yes
- No

Question 3

Am I sold on my idea yet am still having trouble moving forward? Do I find working closely with another person provides motivation and accountability?

- Yes
- No

Constant Action

This chapter has covered clarifying your business intent, breaking down your ideas into actionable chunks, and knowing how to get help with completing those ideas. Now it's time to take that first step and keep walking.

> **"Success loves speed."**
> **~Gary Ryan Blair~**

Taking constant action is vitally important. It builds momentum and excitement and generates wins. Inaction breeds doubt, complacency, and procrastination.

In fact, as my network has expanded to include more and more highly successful people, it has become clear that daily action and daily production is a key differentiator each of them has. They don't produce something great 100% of the time, but even if they produce just 1% of the time, they're still out-producing most everyone.

When I look at people who generate successful businesses, I see them striving to be productive, not perfect. Just like with authors who force themselves to write a certain number of words each day, there seems to be something special about constant production and constant action.

This concept of constant action requires an understanding of what to take action on. Don't be a perfectionist where it doesn't matter. Apply your energy to what really matters and what generates revenue. For everything else, just get it done.

It's time to take everything you've learned in this book and put a huge amount of energy into completing your mind-map actions from earlier in this chapter. Set aside time every day to take action on those goals. Unplug. Wake up early. Perform deep work. Do whatever is needed. Take action.

CHAPTER 12

Going Live

Goals

- Sell Before You're Ready
- Market
- Launch
- Analyze, Tweak, Repeat
- **Action:** Use the daily and monthly worksheets at *justingesso.com/52x*
- **Action:** Take at least one big daily action toward each of your Grinder-3 Goals

Taking a product live means it's time to start receiving money for your business idea. That's exciting. And it's also probably pretty scary. The good news is there is a general template for doing this properly, making money fast, and avoiding many common blunders.

When I made my transition from the corporate world to the entrepreneurial one, it was perhaps the difference in the approach for "going live" that struck me most.

As I already alluded to in the Business Evaluation sections, large companies tend to spend a huge amount of time and effort tweaking and perfecting before launching a product. By contrast, in the startup, side hustle, and entrepreneurial worlds, I learned things are different. People evaluated their concepts and then launched extremely quickly.

I initially thought this was a sure-fire recipe for disaster and that I'd be able to bring my experience in to improve this process, but I hadn't seen the whole picture yet. Once the product is live and these smaller companies were making money, the heavy lifting began. Tweaks, adjustments, and constant improvement became the obsession. The difference was this occurred *after* the launch.

I've come to appreciate this approach. You get to market before your competitors. You make money much earlier in the process. You test real-world ideas, not boardroom ideas. And if done properly, you don't anger customers with lame products and services...rather, you engage them and build champions. I've also come to see how the best of both worlds can be married.

Your Launch Plan

This chapter dives in deep, but here's an overview to give you the big picture:

- **Step 1:** Sell before you're ready. You'll run an amped-up beta, earning money and gaining ever-critical market feedback.
- **Step 2:** Build your marketing machine. People are your lifeline. People give you money. You need a scalable system to nurture relationships, build your brand, and establish trust.

- **Step 3:** Launch! In order to stand out in the crowded marketplace, you are going a hit the scene with a major bang. No knocking—let's break down the door.

- **Step 4:** Analyze, tweak, and repeat. Here's where you'll find the metrics that matter and press on them until you have the desired result.

Step 1: Sell Before You're Ready

Whether your business sells a product or service, and whether it's online or brick-and-mortar, we're going to launch. We're going to get you on the scene with a bang. You're going to leave your mark from Day 1. But before we can do this, we need to refine, tweak, and gain real-life feedback. Every—I repeat every—business idea I've been a part of has changed drastically as soon as it's seen the light of day.

> "We can assume outcomes one way or another, but until we put a method and data behind it to test those assumptions, we're risking being pulled into something that seems right, but may prove to be completely wrong."
> ~Pat Flynn, Will It Fly?~

This, of course, assumes your business actually sees the light of day. Two major problems hold businesses back from ever launching:

- The business owner (you) never takes enough action to actually launch the business. The idea remains nothing more than an idea.

- The owner does take enough action but creates something that no one else wants. It's dead on arrival.

The solution to both of these problems is to sell *before* your product or service is ready. You'll hold your feet to the fire and gain real-world feedback.

This is commonly referred to as beta testing, but the word "beta" isn't wide enough in scope to convey the power of the "sell before ready" principle. Betas are typically used to test completed products. I want real feedback baked in much earlier. And, betas are typically free. I want you to *sell* before you're ready. That implies money is coming in. You will generate real profit now...before you're ready to launch. In order to get true feedback, your customers need their money in the game too. So let's get to it.

An example of "sell before you're ready"

In order to paint the picture a little better for you, let me provide an example. Imagine you plan on selling a 12-step online course for people wanting to improve their website's search-engine results. You've applied this to your own sites and have seen the results. You've completed the content for steps 1 through 3 (of 12). What if you started selling the product now before finishing steps 4 through 12?

Let's imagine...

You sell to your first customer and provide them with step one. But you don't stop there. You sell to a few other customers with different types of sites. They operate in different industries. Some are local businesses; some are purely online. They also have varying levels of experience.

Each step takes one week, and you'll ensure future steps will be ready on schedule. Since they're early adopters, you will personally be engaged to help them apply what they've learned, get the most out of your program, and improve their search engine results.

You now find yourself on the hook to complete additional steps to stay ahead of the customers. Additionally, you will see how well they understand your material, what questions they have, and where they struggle. You'll get an idea of whether or not you're actually solving real problems that other people face.

I expect your plan for steps 4 through 12 will quickly go out the door and you'll have significant adjustments to make. You will take feedback from these customers and apply broader market research to validate significant changes in direction. But this rework is okay...your excitement is growing as you see real results posting and you gain much broader insight and expertise.

Further, you find new ways to get specific. Remember, getting specific is a key to beating the competition and carving out your niche. You find your product works very well for people who are new to search engine optimization and are running a small, local business. Further, you find that once people see the value of naturally ranking highly in results, they are willing to spend much more money with you (whether through follow-up consulting or otherwise).

Alright, what just happened as a result of selling before you're ready?

Well first and foremost, *you actually finished your product!* Rather than giving up 60% of the way through, you actually finished it. And you finished much quicker than you expected.

And here are other outcomes of selling before you were ready:

- Improved and tweaked content.
- Narrowed target audience, which will make marketing easier.
- Uncovered countless new problem statements—new problems your product solves.
- Posted real-world results and gained customer testimonials. One of your customers tripled their leads thanks to you.
- Discovered your product is just the start of a much deeper (and financially rewarding) relationship with customers.
- Determined your target audience will likely spend $299 on an introductory course. Some portion of these buyers will actually apply everything from your course, see results, and be willing to spend $5,000 for a consulting engagement.
- Analyzed your refined market and conservatively determined that by selling two per day, you will make $218,270 per year. With 1% of your course customers, you'll book an additional $5,000 for consulting, which will primary be used as an opportunity to generate new ideas, adapt to the market, and build out your product ecosystem. Adding $218,270 (product sales) to $36,500 (consulting sales), you're sitting on a cool $254,770. Now you're really motivated!
- Booked a consulting client and realized you can make a massive difference in people's lives.
- And...you made money before your product was done!

Ultimately, by going through this exercise, you discovered your little course is not some side hobby or gimmick. It's the center of a real business. It solves real customer problems. You feel excited and proud. You offer tremendous value. Let's make sure you get it in as many hands as possible!

I took this approach while writing this book. I signed up several coaching clients at the same time. I used content from this book as my week-by-week coaching activities and exercises. I gained all of the benefits listed above and ended up completely trashing my initial outline for Parts II, III, and IV. I tackled the book with much more enthusiasm and passion. I was forced to write and progress more quickly than my clients. And I now have something I know delivers outstanding results when applied.

"Sell before you're ready" applies to more than just products

It's generally easy to imagine this concept with products, but it applies equally well to services. Don't have a website? Don't have your invoicing, letterhead, company name, or service offerings figured out? Sell before you're ready.

If you want to start an editing business, for example, reach out to your network and find a few people who are producing content. Offer to edit for them for a great price. In exchange, uncover what they expect of editors. Have your name listed as "Editor" in their publication. Build your portfolio and your understanding of the game. Your preconceptions may not be in line with what today's market truly needs.

I have a friend who started a marketing company with the idea of helping local business generate leads through Facebook and

Google. While local business owners were very interested in this idea, my friend found they really didn't have the right marketing structure in place to receive and properly handle leads. Because of this, the generated leads weren't "working out," and business owners felt they were throwing money away.

The reality is these local businesses needed services starting at a much more rudimentary level. Fortunately, he sold before he was ready. Rather than having a business that was dead on arrival, he was able to adjust his business plan and now sells "marketing engine" websites rather than leads. Once his customers have the right types of websites and lead-handling processes in the back end, they can transition to the longer-term service of generating leads. And as it turns out, websites are easier to sell. The ongoing lead-generation services are a natural progression, especially after the relationship is established and trust is built through the website creation process. While his initial idea sounded great, he found his local customers weren't ready for it. Gaining real-world feedback allowed him to pivot on a dime and adjust.

> "It sounds silly, but I see too many people make these same mistakes when they start their businesses. They put all this time, effort, energy, and money into building a website to be 'open for business.' They're buying into the 'build it and they will come' theory, but this isn't Field of Dreams."
> ~Nick Loper, Buy Buttons~

Waiting until you have everything lined up is a sure-fire way to go the wrong direction, spend unnecessary money, be out of touch with your customers, and be much more likely to fail. The best business owners I know apply this "sell before you're ready" concept on an ongoing basis. They have that startup mentality, which causes them to constantly experiment, be dynamic, and adapt regardless of what they're selling.

There is a time and a place to be perfect and professional, but that needs to be kept in balance and in check. While the big dogs are spending months planning, going through governance committees, and going through final sign offs, you can be out with real customers, making real money, adapting to the real world, and refining as you go.

To whom do you sell?

Alright, you can't sell unfinished products and services to just anyone. You need to sell to people who have some degree of trust in you. Go back to your 52x Business Evaluator work. Remember the "Customer" section? You wanted to start a business in an area that has potential customers who already have a good relationship with you, need what you're offering, and are readily accessible.

You need to be able to talk to them, describe what you're doing, and sell to them. Having a website or fancy flyer won't matter. They trust you. They know you're sold on the idea. They know they'll benefit from it, and they know you'll execute. By providing them value, they'll gladly help you improve, grow, and ultimately market your business via testimonials and documented results.

As your business matures, you can begin applying what you've learned to acquire colder and colder leads. But initial selling will be done to warm leads...leads from your network.

And who knows—as you grow, the number of people who trust you to deliver may expand massively. Elon Musk, leveraging the might of his charismatic-visionary persona, raised approximately $700,000,000 (nearly $1B) by selling deposits for Tesla's yet-to-be-released Model 3 car, of which the details were far and few between. Many people bought before they even saw the unveiling. If you have a great vision and you are sold on it, people who trust you will buy. It's that simple.

What else did Elon Musk create? Brand champions. If you're delivering something awesome and you've engaged customers in part of the creation process, they will naturally become personally attached to your idea. They will *want* to see you succeed. It's human nature, and it's amazingly powerful. If you have a hard time relating to Elon Musk, think about it in terms of a puppy. Raising a puppy is a major pain involving sleepless nights, biting, accidents, and torn-up couches. But going through that phase creates an incredibly strong bond. The same goes for business ideas. As your first customers watch you evolve and go through this transformation, they will become bonded...they will become your champion. Nurture these relationships, overdeliver to them, and keep them close. They will undoubtedly help you grow your business for years to come.

What are your goals?

Selling before you're ready isn't an excuse to be lazy or unprofessional. You do need a specific set of goals for this step. You also need to be upfront with your customers about what you're doing and what you'll be getting out of it.

Each situation varies, but here's a good start:

- Make money. You must prove that people are willing to pay you and that you can operate profitably.
- Provide number-based results achieved by your customers as a result of using your product or service.
- Gain testimonials you can publish.
- Understand real-life customer problem statements.
- Refine your target customers.
- Uncover new angles and ideas for add-on products/services.
- Document a delivery plan.
- Have customers review marketing collateral (website, logos, flyers, etc...).
- Develop a brand champion.

Ultimately, achieving these goals should mean you're ready to go big with your business.

Exercise – Your Customers and Your Goals

On a sheet of paper, write out two lists:
- 20 people to whom you can sell before you're ready.
- 20 goals you specifically have for selling before you're ready.

Step 2: Marketing Machine

I'm about to open a serious can of worms by bringing up marketing. I could easily fill an entire book on the subject and still miss major aspects. But, it's a critically important topic when it comes to successfully selling your service or product, whether online or locally. And it's key to launching, so I need to cover some fundamentals.

Marketing exists to create awareness and trust. Without awareness and trust, selling is an uphill battle. With awareness and trust, people suddenly start saying "yes" much easier and even begin buying proactively. Fortunately, if you are genuine in your business and marketing, awareness and trust are surprisingly easy to build.

This begs the question: if no one knows your or your company, how do you go about building trust? Repetition. Repetition is key to building trust. Simply seeing an image of a company over and over causes you to begin trusting that company. It feels comfortable and familiar. As a result, you feel good about exchanging your money for it. These feelings compliment the rational decision-making process.

Think about your own buying decisions. Which products do you choose? If you check your behavior, I'll bet it's the ones you see, hear, and read about most frequently.

We all know the company Coca-Cola. In fact, much like "Xerox" and "Kleenex," the word "Coke" is often used to mean soda. They are so well branded their company name is a substitute for the entire competitive space. We're already plenty aware of Coca-Cola, so why do they need to continually bombard us with advertising? These constant ads reinforce trust at a subconscious level. Even if you don't want one, you may see a Coke while waiting at a checkout and grab it without thinking. This probably doesn't happen with competitors' products. Indeed, this is why

Coca-Cola continues to spend a whopping $3.4 billion per year on advertising (*Investopedia*).

As an aside, I'm looping back on some concepts I raised in the affirmations portion of this book. If you're not yet making bigger, better decisions and believing you can dramatically alter your life, your self-advertisements aren't up to par. They should be working as hard as Coca-Cola's ads, directing you where you need to go. Take what you learn from this section, and revise your affirmations.

Seven components of a complete marking engine

Since awareness and trust require volume, we need systems to keep your marketing efforts efficient. Your system needs to enable easy communication, interaction, and capturing of customer data. Here, I'll provide a list of the fundamentals that apply to pretty much any type of business. You will need to do further research on each, though, to become an expert.

1. Website

Having a website sounds pretty obvious, right? The reality is most people get it wrong. It may seem simple, but many people don't understand how a website fits into the bigger marketing picture. Websites need to be much more than an online billboard. Websites allow you to capture contact information from leads and remarket to them. Because of this, any marketing effort starts with a proper marketing website.

As you'll see, in order to market to people in a highly cost-effective manner, getting people on your turf—your website—and capturing their information is extremely important. Since websites can facilitate a longer-term relationship with potential customers, even offline marketing (postcards, flyers, etc...) should direct people back to your site.

2. Customer database

You need a way to track meaningful information about customers and prospects. This is commonly called a CRM (Customer Relationship Management) tool. CRMs allow you to track contact information, notes, and where people are in the buying process. It can be as simple as a spreadsheet to start. I personally use *Hubspot*. It's very similar to Salesforce, but its core features are completely free.

3. Lead magnet

When people make it to your website, there needs to be a way to identify interested visitors and collect their contact information. The best way to do this is to offer a free resource related to your product or service. You provide this resource in exchange for their contact information. It can be a free PDF, market report, or whatever is applicable to your business. It should be interesting and valuable to your customer base.

4. Email marketing

Sending email is one of the most effective ways to build your brand, engage your customers, and transform leads into buyers. Even when people don't open your email, they see your name, which slowly but surely lays the foundation of trust. Email marketing tools and services allow you to write one email and have it sent to your people database in a personalized manner. These services also keep you compliant with spam laws and regulations. I use *GetResponse*.

5. Autoresponder

While this is a feature of most email marketing solutions, it deserves its own mention. As you generate leads, you will want to send a series of communications that come at predetermined intervals. These emails are crafted to deliver specific messaging over time to introduce people to your business. These emails create awareness through their content and trust through their frequency. They should also encourage replies and interaction so that you can move on to more meaningful, personal communication. Ultimately these emails will ask the lead to take an action and make a purchase.

6. Social media

Social media is a broad term that really encompasses web-based communication. Just like postcards and email, social media is another chance to get your word out and direct people back to your website. The problem is there are countless social media options, and standing out on any individual platform, let alone many of them, takes serious time and money.

With flashing lights and distractions galore, it's easy to spend time on social media at the expense of higher-value tasks. "Likes don't pay the bills" is a *StartupVitamins* saying I love. Don't pursue social media for the sake of social-media stats. Rather, find a platform that allows you to meaningfully connect with potential buyers. Focus on one or two platforms, do them well, and either let the rest be automated, leveraging tools such as *Buffer*, or ignore them.

While there is a lot of great automation that can be achieved with your marketing machine, I want to give a big warning. Automation can be a double-edged sword. Messaging that works for one set of people on one platform may not work for the next. Ensure you understand your audiences. Then, segment them and adjust messaging accordingly. Additionally, your marketing machine is a supplement—not a replacement—to actual personal interaction.

7. Paid marketing

Paying for marketing online helps you do two different things: reach new people and reinforce your brand.

Let's start with reaching new people. As soon as you look at the advertiser's view of Facebook or Google, you will be floored by exactly how much those platforms know about individuals. These platforms collect data and analyze behavior. As a result, marketers can show ads to very specific audiences in a cost-effective manner. If your target audience is within a three-year age range, lives in a one-mile radius, and is interested in basket weaving and walking their dog, guess what. You can probably show them an ad. Paid ads going after very specific characteristics and interests are how you can drive traffic into your marketing machine.

Next, paid marketing allows you to inexpensively reinforce your brand with anyone who has visited your website or otherwise entered your marketing machine. Have you ever visited a website or searched for a product then begun seeing ads for that brand *everywhere*? This is remarketing at work, and you can easily do it yourself through Facebook, Google, and others. When layered with social media and email, you can achieve Coca-Cola quantities on an average-Joe budget.

What's better is remarketing can be tailored to the customer's journey. If the customer just visited your website, they can be shown a brand-building ad. If they went to your cart but never checked out, they can be shown a coupon or information about your generous return policy. You can get hyper specific.

The only prerequisite to paid marketing is you need a goal for each ad. What action do you want people to take as a result of seeing the ad? This allows you to tie your advertisements to a dollar value, and you can then calculate return on investment. In fact, Facebook and Google allow you to explicitly enter goals into the system, causing the ads to optimize themselves to maximize goal achievement.

Using your marketing machine to build influence

Once you have a marketing engine up and running, you need to use it to drive something. So let's get to driving conversation and engagement with your audience. You need to be persuasive. And by this, I mean you need effective communication and the ability to help people decide if they should move forward with your business or not. Without persuasive communication, your marketing can fall on deaf ears and simply become noise.

Dr Robert Cialdini put together probably the best framework on this topic in his book *Influence: The Psychology of Persuasion*. Let's have a look at some of these key principles in a modern-day context.

1. Reciprocity

Give to get. People love to help those who have helped them. If your business provides something to people, expect people to provide something back to you. As an example, case studies show that when waiters leave two mints with the bill, their tip increases by an average of 23% (*SenseiMarketing.com*). That's simple and cost effective. For you, a great start can be providing a truly valuable lead magnet. What other value can you provide your potential customers?

2. Commitment

What do you stand for? I love this one—it's about providing a concise vision to your customers to make it clear exactly what your mission is. Everything you do becomes consistent with this commitment. Customers know what to expect and can more easily decide if your business is for them.

Remind people of your commitment regularly. For example, I use "I'm committed to helping you start a business and profit this year." In Chapter 11, you already went through your "Business Commitment" exercise. All you have to do now is consistently remind people of your commitment.

3. Social proof

Customers wonder if they are making a bad choice by selecting your business. Are other people choosing your business? Groupthink, assurance, and security all come into play with human behavior. We are tribal at our core and look to peers before making a decision. This is why Amazon's user reviews are so powerful. By taking the "sell before you're ready" approach, you'll build social proof. Make sure to share it in the form of reviews, testimonials, and case studies.

4. Authority

People want their information from trusted sources, not just anyone. This has become ever more important in recent years as the barriers to creating a business and publishing content have dropped.

As you think about why you're the right person to provide a solution to people, focus on numbers-based results and respected credentials. Be sure your customers are aware of these. Legitimize your personal and business authority.

5. Liking

We all want to connect on a personal level, something that's easy to forget as you build a business! People need to personally connect and want to do business with people they like. This is why I focus so heavily on networking. Make sure you actually like people in your network, showing interest and appreciation. And make sure you share personal information about yourself so that people can build a relationship with you, not just your business.

When your customers see a bit of themselves in you, amazing things can happen. There is a ton of direction on improving your relationships throughout this book, but if you need help, be sure to read *How to Win Friends & Influence People* by Dale Carnegie. The principles in that book work whether communicating in person, by email, or through a social network.

6. Scarcity

We are tribe-oriented beings. But we don't want to be part of just *any* tribe. We want to be part of exclusive, unique tribes. People want to be part of a small group that receives special treatment.

People want to be one of the few helping refine your next product. They even want to pay way more than everyone else to be included in a truly exclusive group. So your offers need to include limited-time, limited-quantity, and premium events. As long as you are genuine in your scarcity and not abusing this concept, you'll unlock different types of customers like never before.

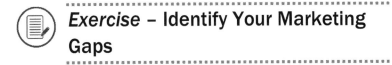

Exercise – Identify Your Marketing Gaps

Alright, let's pull this all together. To have effective marketing, you need a complete marketing machine. It needs to focus on reaching people, capturing contact information, building your brand, and achieving goals. Your messaging and language needs to be consistently checked against the principles of influence. Constantly inspect, test, and revise your communications to better connect with your potential customers and convert more leads into buyers.

Have you considered a marketing plan? How does it line up with what I've described? Do you have the interest and capacity to develop and maintain a marketing machine?

Write down any gaps you have. With this list in mind, consider if you need to reevaluate gaining human help, either through a partnership or otherwise.

Step 3: Launch

Have you noticed the best products never just show up at the store one day? The first trailer for the newest Star Wars film will be released a year before opening day. Drama and gossip trickle into the media over the course of the year. Earned media and online speculation brew. Excitement and anticipation build until you *must* see it not just the week it releases but on the day exact day of release. Yes, you and millions of others wait in line, camp outside, overpay for tickets, and do whatever you can to be part of the launch.

Apple, Tesla, and many others are masters of this concept. Even established businesses like Chick-Fil-A fast-food restaurants don't just show up with new stores—they launch. While I don't eat fast food, I can't help but notice these concepts at play. I'm sure a Chick-Fil-A could simply open the doors of a new store and start making money. But instead, they plaster billboards, take out ads, and mail coupons to thousands of people, all of which advertise "free chicken sandwiches" on opening day. They launch with a bang.

Fortunately, launching plays perfectly into our plan of selling before you're ready. I also want to stress that while launching may seem like a best-practice way to release something, the reality is that it is a *necessity* in today's world. Every day, about 133,000 domains are registered (*Verisign 2016*), 2.7 million blog posts are created (*HostingFacts.com 2016*), and over 6,000 books are published (*Wikipedia, 2017*).

So how do you stand out against this level of constant noise? It's not easy, but the best answer is to concentrate your attack.

Rather than relying on steady marketing, you concentrate everything you have into a single event—your launch. Launching is how you get people talking about your product and service for you. And you'll not only be able to make an impression on humans...you'll also make an impression on machines. These machines and algorithms are the all-important factor when it comes to continuing to be found in the future.

Launches create lasting online effects

The beauty of a launch is that by concentrating your marketing efforts, you will get yourself on the radar in the places that matter. Ranking on places like Google and Amazon will change your life. Whether it's for providing a local service or an online product, if people naturally find you and buy from you, life is easy.

There is practically an exponential curve between ranking and results. Using a book as an example, appearing on page 1 versus page 2 can mean the difference between $20 per month and $500 per month in natural sales. The difference between being search result #1 and result #2 can take you from $3,000 per month to $20,000 per month in natural sales.

I've seen the same principle at work with sales centers in small businesses as well. Small businesses that transition to the front page suddenly see their call centers light up. And it's not a gradual change: Google flipped the switch, and now you're seriously in business!

Simply put, a slow-and-steady approach to marketing doesn't work. You need to blow the doors down and crash onto the scene.

Think about it from Amazon's perspective. Just listing your product "for sale" on Amazon will immediately put you in competition with hundreds of thousands of other products that are *already making money* for Amazon. Why should Amazon bother promoting your unproven product?

On the other hand, what if you put your product on Amazon and then drive 100 or even 1,000 sales on day one? Well, Amazon will make some money, and their algorithms will take notice. You'll earn "hot new release" and "best seller" badges. Why? Because you're generating money for Amazon. You'll move up in the rankings. And then, something magic happens. If you hit the top spots in your category, Amazon suddenly promotes you to their massive customer base who come with wallet in hand. Amazon takes the sales you generated and rewards you by giving you 1,000 times more. And because you're receiving this traffic, your ranking sustains itself.

Ultimately, a competitor will come along with a killer launch and bump you from the top. Or, perhaps the reigning champ muscles its way back over you. But even if you gradually lose your ranking, the lasting effect is real. You've generated real sales. You will start receiving reviews. You'll have lasting power that should keep you on the leaderboard. And most importantly, you've tasted what it's like up top. While your product will continue to rank better than most, you will be fueled to do what it takes to continue edging your way higher because you know how sweet it is up there.

My first book is a great example of this. It was self published and came out of nowhere. No one knew who I was. I was destined to be 1 of 6,000 books published that day, nearly all of which would fall into a black hole. But I knew the importance of *launching*. And I knew the wild ride I'd realize if I could rank up top—even if just for a day.

I did my part to deliver several hundred customers on day one, and sure enough, Amazon took care of the rest. I moved over 12,000 copies that first week. I hit "hot new release" and "#1 bestseller" in multiple countries and ranked in numerous categories. To compare, I know authors who have released excellent books and have sold fewer than 100 copies over many years. Many books never realize a single natural sale. But my book continues to rank thanks to that launch. Even still, I know I can do much better now and have much larger goals for future book launches.

The point is launching creates a buzz. Whether it's on Amazon, Google, or in your local community, coming out with a bang is the only way to get people talking about you. You no longer have to be the only voice shouting your message.

 ## *Exercise* – Schedule Your Launch

Putting a schedule down on paper and committing to it is what will take you from "some day…" to "this is really happening!" And I don't want you to keep your launch to yourself either. One of the best ways to avoid backing out is to announce your launch date. Tell your family and friends. Announce it on social media and to your email list. Commit to a specific date, and then show them how it's done.

Next, use Trello, a sheet of paper on the wall, or a calendar, and map out your launch. As it goes with all big goals, start with the end in mind and work backward. Put the launch date down, then start filling in the blanks back to today. Here's what your mapping should target:

- Identifying free-day giveaway
- Determining discounts and coupons
- Finding five companies for joint marketing
- Finalizing print marketing for flyers, letters, and posters
- Ordering professional artwork and design templates
- Completing welcome-email autoresponder series
- Finalizing keyword research
- Completing ten ad variations
- Completing landing pages
- Finalizing sales-copy editing
- Testing your marketing machine end-to-end
- Turning on Facebook ads
- Getting five testimonials with numbers-based results from pre-launch customers
- Mailing 4,000 postcards
- Making 20 phone calls per day for two weeks ahead of launch
- Etc...
- Launch!

Whether your business is local or online, build a plan that blasts you onto the scene. Inspire your customers. Shock your competitors. Force yourself to deliver.

Step 4: Analyze, Tweak, and Repeat

Woohoo! You've launched your product or service. Congratulations! You're in a small, elite club of people who have actually gone out on their own and bet on themselves. You've taken perhaps the biggest step you can possibly take to forge the life you want.

So it's time to head to the beach and watch the money roll in, right?

Well...not quite yet.

When product launches are done right, you'll feel incredibly euphoric. But sooner or later, the buzz will wear off, and sales will slow. Or, perhaps your launch didn't go well at all. Whatever the case, many people at this stage will find serious doubt creeping in.

Do people dislike my idea? Was this all a huge waste of time? Should I have done more research? Who was I kidding—I'm not an entrepreneur...

While only an elite few will launch a business, an even smaller group will successfully sustain one. But it's not because their ideas are bad. No, it's because they don't muscle through this initial lull. And it's going to take muscle and effort. We all start businesses with extremely high expectations, so when initial results are mediocre, you can react one of three ways:

- Give up
- Accept mediocre results (because after all, you're nothing special)
- Push, push, PUSH until you achieve your idea's potential

Each person I know who has built a successful business has done so by being incredibly mentally tough at this stage. They chose option three. In fact, *the single biggest reason* I've seen business ideas grow and make their owners rich is the owner's persistence during the lull.

As I expanded my network to include more and more business owners—and more and more very successful ones—patterns became very clear, which you have seen throughout this book. But nothing stood out more as "the it factor" than the ability to power through the initial stages of a live business idea.

Reading biographies on great business people and even great scientists, you'll see the same quality repeated. Those "overnight" successes and discoveries didn't really happen overnight at all. They applied obsessive thought and action to ensure their business progressed in the early stages. And that's what you're going to do too.

Your business is a newborn

The best way to think about this stage of your business is to think in terms of a human baby. Your launch was the birth. Everyone came to see it. They showered you with gifts. You looked into your business' eyes and melted. You never felt better!

But now? Now you've slid deep into the reality of raising an infant. You're stressed, questioning yourself, and losing sleep. Everyone is giving you advice.

Just like new parents, most new-business owners freak out during this stage. Just know it's temporary and manageable as long as you focus on the *right stuff.*

Is it worth fighting for?

Here's the good news: this entire book was building up to this section. Every exercise you've done is in your back pocket. The entire outline was worked backward from this moment.

- What lifestyle do you want? What is your personal mission? What are your goals and values? What's your master plan for life? Your business will get you there.

- What success foundation have you built? Who in your network is here to support you right now (you're not alone in this!)? What time and money did you sacrifice in pursuit of this dream? What will you do anything to avoid? Your business is built on too strong a foundation to falter.

- How did you select your business? You know the exceptional potential it has! You know you have customers. You know how to gain an edge with competitors. And you know what will cause money to flow. You've done the analysis. All that's left is you.

And don't forget what's possible! You analyzed competitors. You know your business can succeed at high levels. In fact, you know you can surpass them. It's time to close your eyes, take a breath, and make it happen.

Incremental versus evolutionary gains

As you dive into Step 4, you'll want to be aware of and target two types of changes: incremental and evolutionary. Both are valuable, and often, you don't know which type of change will occur until it happens. But being aware that both types of change exist is critical so that you don't overlook an opportunity.

Incremental gains are tweaks that improve sales or profitability in a stair-step fashion. Say your baseline is 20 sales per month. By utilizing Google Optimize to test wording variations on your website, you were able to improve your landing pages and move up to 23 sales per month. This was an easy change that didn't cost you anything but a little time.

Similarly, you run Facebook Ad variations, targeting two completely different sets of interests and demographics. Wow had you missed the boat initially! You found the right audience, which was fairly different than you initially expected. Over the last few weeks, your opt-in rates have quadrupled, and your sales moved up to 35 per month.

Finally, you take this updated wording from your initial website tests and apply it to your Facebook ads. You run tests there to ensure the same messaging helps your ads perform better. It does, driving traffic to your site at half the cost. Your newly doubled traffic jumps you up to 50 sales per month.

While you had a great product, you weren't targeting the right people, and therefore, the right people weren't getting to your site. Further, many of "the right people" misunderstood your business, didn't think it was for them, and left. But now you uncorked your potential. You're targeting the right people, and those people understand your value. This is an extremely common scenario and can really only be tackled once your business is in the wild collecting real-world data. This example shows how three incremental gains can snowball into doubling your business relatively easily.

Evolutionary gains, on the other hand, are large moves that fundamentally change the business model or offering. You may make huge change in pricing, your sales channels, or you may introduce a new product. Maybe only tens of people want to pay $199 for your information as a course. But, thousands of people want to pay $12.99 for it as a book. You do the math, and it's better to release your content as a book.

These evolutionary changes may not even be the result of lackluster sales. You might have one entry-level product that is selling extremely well, and you find people who bought it are yearning for more. They want more depth, and they're willing to pay for it.

The point of this section is to be aware that you can look at your business from two different levels, and both are important. Incremental gains are generally easier to find and implement. As such, numerous incremental gains can have the same effect as one evolutionary gain. So don't shy away from them, but don't spend all of your time in the weeds either. Regularly looking at the big picture is extremely important. It will ensure you understand the competitive landscape, your customers, and how your business can continue to succeed in the future.

One last note. You will likely find many incremental gains yourself, but evolutionary gains generally originate from *other people*. This is why you need to brainstorm with your network. You need to talk to your customers. You need to shop the competition. You need to be out in the field. Don't get stuck behind a computer screen—interact with other people constantly. Big changes require fresh and alternate perspective.

How to apply the right pressure

It's time to knock your business idea out of the park and have it achieve its potential. You have the fuel to power through this stage. But how do you make the right moves?

When things aren't going quite right, it is common to be distracted by shiny objects. Maybe I need more Facebook Likes. Maybe I need to buy this SEO Guru's Mastermind Program. Or maybe I need chatbots! Actually, all this new stuff is overwhelming. I'm going to bury my head in all this tax and insurance paperwork. That sounds easier.

The better answer is you need to find the right metric and get ready to press hard on it. You need to analyze, tweak, and repeat. And you'll do this until you have your desired result.

So what do I mean by the right metric? This metric is the variable that needs to change in order for your business to generate more cash without causing conflict with your lifestyle goals.

To start, go back to your Business Evaluator Phase 4. Review how you expected your business idea to make money. What was the unit? Now, it's a matter of brainstorming which activities will truly move this number in the right direction. Out of your list, you'll want to pick the *top three activities* and determine how much each activity should influence your metric on a percentage basis.

You now have, as a business owner, your action plan to make things happen. For the next two weeks, you will spend 80% of your work time on these three activities, proportional to their influence. That's right, 80% of your time needs to be focused on just three activities. Paperwork, bookkeeping, and other distractions take a back seat. Focus on three activities that will directly influence your success metric.

Apply measures to these activities so you can actually make the right tweaks. If I make 100 calls per week at 3% conversion rate, I'll hit my goal. This allows you to try three different approaches (or scripts) and measure which converts better. Do any of these approaches allow me to hit that 3%, which means I hit my goal? Do any of these approaches double that so I only have to make 50 calls to achieve the same result?

Analyzing, tweaking, and repeating is not just about applying action and pressure. It's about testing, measuring, and progressing your business smartly. You are figuring out what makes an *actual* difference in the results that matter. Get scientific.

Business owners commonly get lost in activities that don't matter. There is an endless array of non-value-add work to keep you occupied. But if that's where your focus is, your value diminishes. And people pay for value. So rather than falling into this trap, keep that metric front and center. Constantly focus on the activities that will influence it.

How will you know these are the right activities? You won't at first. But that's why you have a measurable target. If you work hard and consistently (80% of your time) on these three activities over the next two weeks, yet you don't see a change in the results for your metric, you likely don't have the right activities. That's okay and is part of the process. Go back and pick new activities. Consult with your network. Dive deep.

This approach will ensure you work on the *right* things. You're not working on paperwork, busy work, or shiny work. This is the time in your business' lifecycle when you have to put it all on the table and work on what matters to keep your business alive and make it thrive. Apply massive activity. Apply massive pressure. As a result, you will figure out what to tweak. You will figure out which tasks move the needle.

And here's the good news: once you figure out how to move the needle, you have the ability to systematically grow your business. You can automate or hire someone to press on these tasks for you. Maybe you don't like performing the activities that truly make your business grow, but that doesn't mean you'll be stuck doing them. As the business owner, it's your responsibility to uncover them. Then you can hand them off to someone who enjoys and excels at those activities.

Don't forget to repeat

If you spend your time during your business's infancy working on what moves the needle, you will quickly find yourself with an amazing, growing business. But don't stop there. Apply continuous improvement to your business. Once you uncork one metric, select a new metric to press on and improve. Markets change. Customers change. Communication changes. Successful businesses change. You need to constantly inspect, adapt, and improve.

This is the principle of "working *on* the business" instead of "working *in* the business." Real success and gratification comes when the business owner works on selling and improving.

Go back to the time exercises, which you applied to your personal life. Do these exercises again but in the context of your *new* life. Eliminate, delegate, and automate as much as possible in your business so that you don't get sucked into a trap of your own creation. After all, your business is here to serve you and your lifestyle, not the other way around.

Exercise – Analyze, Tweak, Repeat

- What metric most needs to change in order for your sales and profit to improve? It's okay to start simple with "monthly sales."
- What three activities are most likely to change this number?
- Rank and allocate a percentage of estimated influence to each of these activities. For example: 60% for activity one, 30% for activity two, and 10% for activity three. This means that during your "working on the business" time, you'll spend 60% of your time on activity one.
- Over the next two weeks, spend 80% of your work time on these three activities according to their influence weighting. Spend the remaining 20% of your time working on things you *need* to work on, such as paperwork. Go all in on these activities.
- Keep a close eye on your metric. Take notes. Capture data. Figure out the numbers behind these activities and how they drive your metric.
- Depending on your results, keep at it or change up your activities. Brainstorm. Get people involved. Get your business serving you.

If you're struggling with this, I'd love to brainstorm with you. I first learned these "analyze, tweak, and repeat" principles back in my corporate days, namely through Kaizen and Six Sigma trainings. And boy did I soak it in. This is an area at which I excelled. It allowed me to make huge changes at big companies. It has since helped me get where I am today and help many others with their small businesses. At the end of the day, this is a numbers game that requires a certain type of creativity. If it isn't clicking for you yet, just shoot me an email at justin@justingesso.com, and let's make it happen together.

BONUS CHAPTER

Going Big

Is your business idea blowing your expectations out of the water? Do you feel the world is primed for more? Before I close this book, I want to provide some insight on taking things to the next level. You have numerous options for going big with your idea, some of which you can do without adding much risk.

While having a bunch of income from your business is fantastic, it's no guarantee you'll generate big wealth and big level-jumps on your own balance sheet. Within my network, I have numerous people playing at the million-dollar level. They're doing million-dollar deals and acquiring multi-million-dollar assets. But they didn't get to that position based on their admittedly large monthly cash flow. Rather, they went big at some point in their journey.

Luck, Experience, and Guts

Going big is a mixture of luck, experience, and guts. Luck means being in the right place at the right time. Experience means having the understanding to know it's actually the right place and right time. And guts means actually doing something about it.

It's the combo that takes you big.

As an example, one of my friends has done this twice in real estate. He is a licensed real estate agent who doesn't enjoy working with typical buyers and sellers. As such, he began doing work for banks. He became a vendor, went through their onboarding processes, and then began grabbing tasks that these banks put into a pool for all qualified vendors. These tasks might be valuing, taking pictures of, or inspecting properties. They weren't high paying, but for my friend, they beat working with traditional buyers and sellers.

But, when the housing market crashed, suddenly these same banks had a ton of houses to sell. They pushed listing contracts out to the same vendors. A ton of them. The old tasks may have paid around $75 each. Listings, on the other hand, paid thousands.

While other real estate agents scrambled to become vendors with these banks and get the listings, my friend faced a supply-and-demand problem that greatly favored him. The other real estate agents who were already in the system benefited too, but like most agents, they only felt comfortable taking two to three listings at a time.

My friend was different. He realized how big this opportunity was. He went big. See, luck had put him in this position. His experience told him this financial crisis wasn't a small deal. He knew it was just the start. And he had the guts to go big. Instead of just assigning two to three deals to himself, he grabbed every possible one. In order to fulfill them, he hired assistants and went to work. He had as many as 60 listings at one time. That's about 30 times what a normal agent would consider doable. He went big and launched his career as a result.

This same agent went big again shortly thereafter. With housing prices at a major low (luck), he began seeing signs of prices bottoming out (experience). He took action (guts) by buying houses. When most other investors were dumping their rentals, my friend began buying them up. Where most people would be faced with incredible uncertainty and would maybe buy one or two properties, he bought as many as possible. He used his own cash, asked family for money, and hit up any bank that would lend to him. He went big, the market more than recovered, and life became amazing.

I have personally seen similar moves within the tech industry, with assets in India, in currency, and even in simple Internet-based businesses. Every "making it big" story has the same three ingredients: luck, experience, and guts.

My goal here is to provide you with the foresight and perspective to take action when luck strikes you. With that said, here are some mechanisms for getting the money to go big.

Business Loans

The first thing most people think of when considering going big is obtaining a loan. This includes small-business loans, investment loans, and personal loans.

The problem is debt and interest scares people. Running a business is risky. Going big on a business is riskier. Without a loan as a safety net, having your business collapse is terrible. It hurts your pride and eats up whatever you've personally invested into the business. But what if you were also saddled by huge debt? Do you lose way more than just your business?

For this reason, people are often wary of taking on debt to build their business. However, it is also one of the best and most readily available tools to push your proven business model to the next level. Going back to your *52x Business Evaluator Phase 4*, you have a framework for figuring out your net profit. With a loan, you simply add a couple of new expense lines which are "loan payback" and "interest expense." This is called debt service, and it is simply viewed as line items in your business case.

By taking on debt, you should also expect to increase revenue. So after entering the new expenses, you account for the top-line changes that result from this loan. The loan should multiply your earnings. Perhaps you increase your expenses by a factor of 1.2x but increase your income by a factor of 20x.

Seen this way, a loan is really no different than marketing expenses or an office lease. It's a necessary part of running your business, and as long as your cash flow covers it, the model makes sense.

The question becomes—what if my business falls apart? What if I lose my income? The answer depends on the type of loan and your situation. The problem is most people don't know the answer, so they assume the worst. The only way you can answer this question is to go sit down with and talk to a few lenders. And you must to do this before you *need* a loan. Educate yourself up front.

Thinking of debt in terms of an expense item and also considering worst-case scenarios allows you to manage the risk of taking out a loan. Think about it. You probably wouldn't second guess taking out a mortgage for an investment property. Your property is a business, and you're getting a loan for it. In fact, for every $1 you put into the deal, traditional banks easily hand over $5 to let you go big. Why aren't you concerned? Because you know how mortgages work.

You may have also looked at a spreadsheet that has rental income as a top line. Below, you subtracted the mortgage payment, insurance, taxes, and more. The math works, and you earn monthly profit. Your numbers even show that if the rental demand drops in half, you can still pay the mortgage and get by. And lastly, you know the worst case. Worst case is you lose the house, perhaps because rent demand falls ten times from what it is today, and you can't make the payment. You don't lose your personal house. You don't lose your car. No one takes your kids.

Because you know the numbers and the worst case, you feel comfortable getting home loans.

Business loans are the same. You just need to know your numbers and your options. Once you have these pieces in place, you have an incredible tool for multiplying your business. For every one of your dollars, five dollars are injected into the business. If you are in a position where luck, experience, and guts intersect, loans are a great tool to leverage this position and go big.

Loan options

There are many ways to get loans. You may reach out to friends and family. Or, you may go a more standard route. As you start, here are a few options to explore:

Local banks for business loans

Seek out a local (state or regional) bank, and specifically, a person within that bank who handles business and investment loans. First, local banks are typically the sources of these types of loans. Second, sitting down face-to-face with a lender is hugely valuable. You should plan on bringing a business concept and your spreadsheet with numbers. They will typically plug your numbers into their underwriting tool, which is hugely educational. Over time, you will develop a relationship with this person. The lending can then become about their belief in your ability to succeed in addition to just numbers in a spreadsheet.

SBA loans

The Small Business Administration (SBA) offers programs specifically to help small businesses. The SBA doesn't lend the money themselves. Rather, they provide backing to banks that do loan to small-business owners. This reduces a bank's risk and allows them to lend more freely and at lower interest rates. SBA has incentives for general loans, equipment loans, micro loans, and more. Find a local bank that is an approved SBA lender and you'll gain access to these programs.

Purpose-based loans

Certain lenders specialize in growing specific types of businesses. Whatever your industry or business model, you can research and find investors who understand what you're trying to accomplish and will provide funds accordingly. You may also find your local government is looking to invest in certain types of businesses to grow the city. Through this, you can receive highly incentivized loans or even grants that do not need to be paid back.

Private loans

This category is fairly broad, including loans from family and friends as well as more-formal private sources such as hard-money loans. Many of the business owners I know received their first set of funds from family and friends. Yes, we're back to having a strong network! Friends and family are great because they know and trust your abilities, so they have much more than just a spreadsheet to help them decide if they think you'll succeed. Taking this road has many pros and cons which are too numerous to list here, but consider it and do your research.

Personal loans

Do you just want some extra padding in your life? If you have decent credit, you can probably get a line of credit from your bank right now. They may, for example, give you a $75,000 credit line. You might pay a small fee up front and something like $75 per year. It acts as a checking account in that you can use a debit card, write checks, or otherwise access the funds. If you have a balance, you'll be charged interest, but that rate is typically much lower than the rate on credit cards. Having access to these funds is a great way to be able to act big if you come across a great opportunity. It also gives you some "worst case" funds to dip into during a low month or two. There are many alternatives, like refinancing your house, increasing your credit card limits, and more. Obviously, if abused, there are risks to any of these options, but that's for another book. Most business owners I know have personal lines of credit for the benefits they afford.

Exercise – Talk to Five Lenders

Whether or not you need a loan now, take it upon yourself to go speak to five lenders. Going through this exercise will greatly increase your business-finance savvy. You'll see the questions bankers ask and the models they build.

Most importantly, if you were scared of getting a loan, this exercise will ease your concerns. It will address the two things you need to know:

- What is the actual cost of money to my business?
- What is the worst-case scenario for getting a loan?

As you choose five lenders, ensure you pick a variety. Chat with a couple of local banks. Find SBA lenders. Talk to private-money and specialized lenders. Reach out to your local government to see what programs and planning they have in place to help business owners flourish.

To get you rolling, here are a couple of great resources at SBA.gov:

- *https://www.sba.gov/loans-grants/see-what-sba-offers/sba-loan-programs*
- *https://www.sba.gov/lendermatch*

Limited Partners and Joint Ventures

Alright, I've talked a lot about partnerships in this book, but this is a very different type of partnership. Before, I urged you to use a partnership as a way to gain high-skill talent without the payroll expense. Similarly as beautiful, a limited partnership is about gaining funding. It is similar to a loan, but in my opinion, it's typically the best way to go big on a business idea. Why? You gain all the advantages of a loan...without the risk.

This type of partnership can be referred to as a joint venture, partnership, or joint ownership. There are a variety of specific terms and definitions, but I'll focus on the common elements. Basically, we're looking at a structure that has a managing partner who runs the business and limited partners who provide capital. It is a profit-sharing arrangement.

At a high level, the idea is you see a great business opportunity in front of you. Luck, experience, and guts are all in place. But you need the money. Rather than get a loan, you talk to a couple of people in your network. They are extremely excited about the idea. But they don't want to give you a loan and earn some measly interest. That's boring. No...they want in.

Together with your friends, you go over the numbers and risk. They agree to fund the business. You agree to make the company happen. You form an LLC with you as the Managing Partner and everyone else as Limited Partners. You talk to an attorney to establish the company and operating agreement properly.

What do your friends have? They have ownership in your company. They put in money up front and could potentially earn from your business forever. They gain a percentage of the profits...a percentage of any sale. Their risk is limited to their investment.

What do you have? You have a bunch of cash and a business to go run! It depends on the arrangement, but you typically retain full control of the company and the majority stake. You do not have much financial risk at all—your risk is really your relationship with the limited partners. But hopefully you can manage the relationships and expectations effectively, so this isn't an issue...even if things go wrong.

You will also have to put in your hard work, blood, tears, and sweat while the limited partners get to kick back and watch. But hey, that's okay because you're fulfilling your personal mission, and someone else is willing to fund it.

This concept is very common and extremely advantageous to every person. From a limited partner's side, what other investment has this sort of potential? From the managing partner's side, it is truly all upside. Let's look at the numbers in an example.

Limited partner example

Let's say you have a side-hustle idea mining cryptocurrency. You're technically inclined and have a great storage room in your basement to run a lot of computer gear. You figure a $5,000 investment in hardware will generate an average of $1,000 per month over the next 12 months. It sounds like a killer business!

Further, you believe in the future of cryptocurrency and truly understand the value of its blockchain technology in applications outside of currency. You see big companies getting behind it. Do you have the guts to go big? What if you invested $50,000 and made $10,000 per month? And that's all assuming stable prices. If prices continue to rise, you stand to make huge money. Wow.

But let's look at the downside. You acknowledge this is a very speculative endeavor. It doesn't have the fundamentals of and safety offered by real estate. Although values have been rising incredibly, they could just as easily go down...all the way to zero.

What if new regulations or other unknowns cause a massive downshift? Mining is a supply and demand equation too. While the numbers are great now, what if more miners hit the scene? What if there are fewer transactions or other factors that reduce the need for your computing power?

For you, $50,000 is simply too much to risk. But you also don't want to miss out on the potentially massive upside.

Option 1

Go it alone. Your business investment is $5,000. <u>Your net profit is $1,000 per month</u>.

Now let's consider how this would play out in a limited partnership model. Assume you have four buddies who are very excited about mining. They are very bullish on the concept. But, three of them aren't technically savvy enough to set up and manage their own systems. The fourth doesn't have the space for it.

You all agree to go in as partners. Each of the four become limited partners, investing $9,000 into the business. You are the managing partner, investing $5,000 into the business. You will have sole authority to run and manage the business. You will purchase, set up, and house the equipment. As a result, you get a 50% stake in the business. Each of the remaining four gets 12.5% ownership each.

Option 2

Limited partnership. Your business investment is the same $5,000. <u>Your net profit is $5,000 per month</u>.

How does this work for the limited partners? How have you quintupled your revenue without putting any additional money in? Let's dive in.

The Limited Partners each invest $9,000 in the business and net $1,250 per month. As far as investments go, that is an insane amount! Annualized, that's a 167% return. Where else can you possibly get this sort of return on your money?

Between you and the Limited Partners, there is a total of $50,000 invested into the business. That's ten times the amount if you had gone alone. Likewise, the total revenue is ten times larger.

As a Managing Partner, you increased your income by five, but you didn't increase your risk at all. You don't have debt looming over you. And, you have four friends wanting to see this go well—so that's great accountability.

Notes on limited partnerships

This manner of building a business almost seems too good to be true. You can multiply your earnings without increasing financial risk. Many business owners in my network utilize this method. And the reality is it's a scaled-down version of what almost every major business does: selling stocks. Large companies utilize this model in one way or another. As you apply it to your business, here are a few notes to consider:

- Setting up these types of agreements is typically a one-time event. That means you cannot continually engage new partners to grow the business. Plan properly from the start.

- To form a partnership, you need to engage a corporate attorney. It's a fairly standard exercise, so it isn't expensive.
- Joint ventures and partnerships are different than raising capital. Selling equity, stocks, and debt are specifically governed activities. These are not what this section is talking about.
- There are countless variations and similar constructs. For example, I'm currently working on buying a large apartment complex, and we are using a similar model to do so. However, the naming and requirements are slightly different. But as far as I care, those are just details for the attorneys to worry about.

Exercise – Joint Ventures and Your Business

As you read through the example above, did it spark any thoughts for your business? If so, call an attorney friend to explore the concept. If you don't have one, set up an appointment with a local firm. They will typically do free initial consultations. Go through your business plan and gain a better understanding of how you can apply this model to your business.

Other Ideas for Growing Your Business

I've discussed the two main ways to grow your business: loans and partnerships. These are the two ways I've leveraged my money to grow my businesses. But there are countless other options out there. In fact, "creative finance" is an entire discipline on its own. Here are other common methods you can explore:

- Regulation D fundraising (selling stocks and bonds)
- Venture capital and angel investors
- Local government grants (mentioned briefly in the loan section)
- Crowdfunding on sites such as *Kickstarter*, *Indiegogo*, or *Go Get Funding*
- Universities commonly fund innovative business ideas, especially for alumni
- Your 401(k) can also be used—if you think you can do better with your retirement account than Wall Street can

Whatever your situation, don't limit yourself to your money! Get creative with financing. If I limited myself to the cash I had when I quit my job, I would not have made it anywhere near this far. Loans and partnerships have been critical to every major business opportunity I've pursued. If you feel great about a business idea, go big!

Final Thoughts

Wow, we've covered a lot of ground! My sincere hope is you're inspired to begin crafting your own life and generating money on your own. I believe this book gives you everything you need to successfully generate, evaluate, and execute on business ideas you love.

But it has also undoubtedly caused you to think of many questions I didn't address or anticipate. I want you to keep your momentum going, and I'll be happy to discuss those ideas with you. So please don't hesitate to contact me at justin@justingesso.com.

You can also find me at:

- *facebook.com/justingesso*
- *twitter.com/justingesso*

Also, watch for continuous updates at *justingesso.com*.

About the Author

Justin Gesso holds an MBA and had a good run in corporate America. He was able to make the leap to working on multi-million-dollar startups while also pursuing numerous other exciting projects and investments. He authored the bestselling book *Leave the Grind Behind* to capture this experience and enable others to follow their dreams.

Along with solid achievements in the professional arena, Justin has also been able to maintain a personal life rich in family, health, and community.

Justin has been practicing and refining the principles you'll see in this book for over a decade. These practices are the result of reading hundreds of books and having some of the best professional and personal coaches in the world.

Within just one-and-a-half years of quitting his day job, Justin was able to double his six-figure income. Within two years, he doubled his net worth. He has realized repeated success in multiple business ventures, defying the startup failure rate.

None of this would be possible on the *standard* path. In order to achieve these goals, Justin had to leave the grind behind.

Acknowledgements

A lot of hands are in this book.

My readers supplied the motivation to write. Thank you for sharing your support and success stories.

My entrepreneurial and hustler friends fueled me with ideas. Thank you for jointly working on ways for us to level up.

My parents laid the foundation. Thank you for your unconditional love, guidance, and support.

My wife kept me focused on the big picture. Thank you for your loving approach and for making certain I get the most from all aspects of life.

My son lit the creative fire. Thank you for keeping me on my toes, ensuring I laugh, and constantly wondering why I haven't finished this book yet.

One Last Thing

Allow me to ask you a favor. If you enjoyed this book and feel your life has improved as a result...

Give a copy of *The Book on Small Business Ideas* to a friend or family member.

Help from people like you is how I can achieve my ambitious goal of improving the lives of *millions*. I hope you set a similar goal.

Best regards and thank you,

Justin Gesso